Fast Money

Fast Money

7 Days to Successful Options Trading

Victor R. Napier

iUniverse, Inc.
New York   Lincoln   Shanghai

Fast Money
7 Days to Successful Options Trading

Copyright © 2008 by Victor Napier

iUniverse books may be ordered through booksellers or by contacting:

iUniverse
2021 Pine Lake Road, Suite 100
Lincoln, NE 68512
www.iuniverse.com
1-800-Authors (1-800-288-4677)

Because of the dynamic nature of the Internet, any Web addresses or links contained in this book may have changed since publication and may no longer be valid.

The information, ideas, and suggestions in this book are not intended to render professional advice. Before following any suggestions contained in this book, you should consult your personal accountant or other financial advisor. Neither the author nor the publisher shall be liable or responsible for any loss or damage allegedly arising as a consequence of your use or application of any information or suggestions in this book.

ISBN: 978-0-595-45729-8 (pbk)
ISBN: 978-0-595-90029-9 (ebk)

Printed in the United States of America

Contents

Foreword

Marvin W. Turner, JD MBA RFS CWM CAM CFS

Principal, Black Arrow Advisors, Inc. and Adjunct Professor of Finance

I am delighted to write a forward for the book, 7 Days to Successful Stock Options Trading for Victor Napier.

As a former registered representative, former chief financial officer and registered investment advisor, I have worked with both individuals and corporations to design portfolios that meet their particular level of return relative to their acceptable risk. Investors, as a class, have been risk averse, and only take on additional risk when they are compensated for taking that risk. A well balance portfolio, which may consist of equities, fixed income, real estate, cash equivalents, etc., can be adequately protected using derivatives, or instruments that derive their value based on an underlying security. One such derivative is the stock option.

Stock options, as a class, have been used both to leverage returns and to limit downside risk, depending on whether they are "Puts" or "Calls", "naked" or "covered". In many cases they are purchased for portfolio insurance ... in other cases they are purchased prior to quarterly releases in order to leverage the bump from upside earnings surprises. While futures are somewhat known for their seemingly unlimited risk (you remember the movie "Trading Places", don't you?), options traders may limit their risk and, when used correctly, may profit from stocks rising from stocks falling or from stocks trading flat.

Victor has taken both fundamental (think "Warren Buffet") and technical (think "stock charts") analysis, combined it with various action plans, and then tied that in with a basic understanding of market psychology ... and he has written it in a treatise that will provide an excellent read for both "newbies" and for market professionals. In addition, he has shared the strategies for selecting an option to trade and for designing a strategy for success. While no strategy can be guaranteed 100%, following a well thought out strategy can put more "W's" in your win column than "L's".

On another note, I have known Victor for several years and admire his integrity, drive and his willingness to share the wealth of his knowledge of Wall Street with the masses of Main Street.

Introduction

It was written that in 320 B.C., Alexander the Great was the first to go on record as having used options. As the young conqueror and his unstoppable army's overpowered one tribal chieftain after another, Alexander would offer a payment in gold to secure the option to wed any attractive young daughter that a vanquished king might have. That is to say, in the interest of peace and politics (to say nothing of lust), Alexander the Great went on record as having purchased an option to wed and—even in those ancient times—it was considered a contract secured by the acceptance of a payment. Unfortunately, the young king died before he had a chance to exercise any of his options for domestic bliss. Today, thousands of years later, options are one of the fastest growing investment vehicles in the United States and gaining rapid acceptance in many other international markets ... not for the purposes for acquiring future spouses but to make money or to help reduce risk on certain investments.

Today, options are contracts on an underlying trading instrument—shares of stock, bonds, a commodity, real estate, etc. (The list is endless.) But for this book, we will confine our discussion to options on stocks and stock indices traded under the "American system".

Purpose

The purpose of this book is to introduce the curious investor or novice options trader to the exciting potential of stock options and how to get started quickly and successfully trading stock and stock index options on US markets. The title of this book promotes the idea that if you read one chapter each day (and understand it) by the time you finish the last chapter; you'll have enough knowledge to get started successfully trading stock and index options.

When most investors hear the word "option" they usually associate it with "risk". No doubt, an investor can lose money quickly trading in options. But the reason that many get burned is that they lack the intellectual and psychological tools to harness the rewards that risks make possible. As a matter of fact, in some ways, options can be safer than owning stocks and bonds. But let's not twist words or try to make trading options something it is not. There is risk in trading in options. But we ask two questions: 1) why do some people make a lot of money trading options? and 2) why did over 200 million option contracts trade last year?[1]

Are there that many fools out there?

First of all, let's define what an option "trader" is as compared to a stock "investor". A *Trader* is defined as someone who regularly buys something and sells it for a profit within a short period of time. An *Investor* purchases something with the purpose of reselling at a profit after a longer period of time as compared to a *trader*. Most Investment gurus preach due diligence, buy the stock and then be patient. And this strategy has proven—over the long term—to be good advice. But trading is a different matter.

A stock option trader (speculator) not only must analyze the direction of price movement of a security but also the time when movement might occur. The very nature of an option is short term with most options lasting five months. But the magic of leverage makes even small movements—up, down or even sideways—a potential profit. There is no doubt that trading options is not investing in the traditional sense. Does this send shivers up your spine or titillate your interest? If it's the later, read on.

Let me introduce you to what is probably one of the most attractive things about stock options: you can "rent" a large position of the underlying stock for a period of time for pennies on the dollar and risk only the "rent". For example, if you think a stock is going to go up within a certain period, you can "rent" the stock. You don't have to buy it. The same works if you think a stock is going to go down. But get this … if you think the stock wont do a thing, you can make money on that, as well! But we are galloping ahead of ourselves.

Take a look at this simple example:

You think XYZ stock will go up for whatever reasons you may have. Let's say XYZ shares sell for $45 a share. To own 200 shares would cost $9,000 dollars.

---

1   CBOE (Chicago Board of Options Exchange) report for 2005

To "rent" 200 shares might cost as low as $200. If you were correct in your analysis of XYZ and it moves up $3 per share, you would gain $600. In this example we won't consider commissions. You can see from the table below what your return on investment (ROI) would be under the two situations. The leverage you gain from using options provides a 300% return on the premium investment (rent) whereas owning the stock captures a 6.6% return on the investment.

Cost of 200 shares of XYZ at $45 per share	Cost	Profit on move up of $3 @ share	Return on Investment
Ownership	$9000	$600	6.6%
Option	$200	$600	300%

Suppose that instead of going up $3, let's assume that the price goes down $3 and doesn't recover before the end of the option period. The loss would be limited to the $200 premium, no matter how low the stock went.

Cost of 200 shares of XYZ at $45 per share	Cost	loss on move down of $3 @ share
Ownership	$9000	-$600
Option (2 contracts)	$200	-$200

In the case of options, the risk is limited to the cost of the "rent" (premium) for the period. In this case options can be less risky in that there is a clearly defined maximum risk.

A sock option is a derivative of an underlying security; that is, the option is directly affected by what happens to the underlying asset. Options are also a very flexible tool for investors as well as traders. Options can be used as "insurance" to help reduce risk on larger positions (hedging), a way to hold a large position with minimized use of capital (speculation), a method of buying or selling stock and other more arcane situations. This book will focus on trading options using basic strategies. More complex uses of options will be covered in a sequel edition.

CHAPTER 1

Introduction to Options

The classic definition of a stock option is: a contract that gives the holder of the contract the right (not obligation) to purchase or sell a specific amount of underlying asset shares at a specific price if exercised within a certain time period.

An option is also called a derivative in that it derives its value from an underlying asset.

Basic Option Terminology and definitions

- The purchase of a <u>Call</u> contract conveys the right to <u>buy</u> 100 shares of an underlying asset at a specific price anytime before the expiration of the contract period.
- The purchase of a <u>Put</u> contract conveys the right to <u>sell</u> 100 shares of an underlying asset at a specific price anytime before the expiration of the contract period.
- The owner of an option is called the Holder.
- Hedging is when a position is taken in opposition to the underlying asset position. For example, if you are long 1,000 shares of XYZ a long put position would be taken (10 puts). If the stock goes down in price, the value of the put contracts will increase and should help offset the loss of the declining long stock position.
- The purchase of a call or put is considered as having a Long position.
- A person who sells options is said to have a Short position.
- A person who sells rights to an option is also called the Writer.
- One <u>option contract</u> consists of the right to <u>100 shares</u> of the underlying asset.

- A <u>Premium</u> is the amount paid for <u>each share</u> in a contract.
- The <u>Strike Price</u> is the price at which the option can be exercised. For a <u>call</u> option, it is the price that the underlying stock must go <u>above</u>. For a <u>put</u> option, it is the price that the underlying stock must go <u>below</u>.
- <u>Expiration date</u> is the <u>third Friday</u> of the expiration month.

Let's stop here for some basic examples of how Calls and Puts can work to make a profit. The following two examples are the most common types of trades and are called "long positions" in that both options are purchased from a seller.

<u>Example of purchasing a call option</u>: It's February. You live in the Northeast and you heard a knowledgeable uncle say that spring usually brings about an increase in the stock price of Home Depot (HD) due to the seasonality of construction. The current price of HD is $35 a share. You would like to purchase HD stock, but you really can't afford to purchase the stock in any sizeable amount. You have heard about stock options so you decide to call your stock broker to find out more. Your broker tells you that the current price of a May contract of HD with a <u>strike price</u> of 37.50 is priced at a <u>premium</u> of $2.50 a share. One contract is 100 shares so a contract would cost $250. With $500, you can purchase two contracts which will give you "temporary custody" of 200 shares of HD until the third Friday of May (contract month). You ask your broker what the transaction costs (commissions) will be and he says that he will do it for free (in your dreams). So you purchase 2 HD EU-E (the EU-E designates the contract series which has the strike price and expiration month you bought) contracts which will expire on the third Friday of May.

As your uncle had figured, by mid April HD has risen to over $42 per share. Your May options now sell for a <u>premium</u> of $6 per share. You call your broker and have her/him <u>close out your position (sell your contracts)</u>. You make a profit of $3.50 per share ($6–$2.50); you made a net profit of $200 or a 40% profit on the $500 premium in the two months you held your position.

Below is a graphic representation of what happens when a profit is made with a call

Buying a call (long)

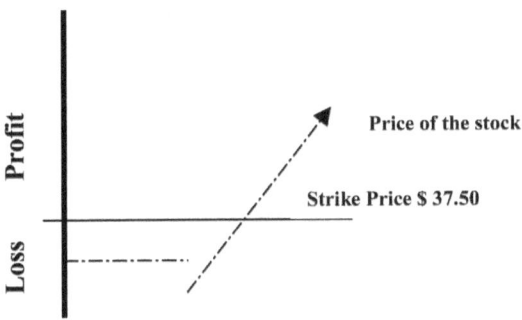

Fig. 1

<u>Example of purchasing a Put option</u>: It's now September and you believe that the price of HD will go down as winter approaches. The <u>current price of HD is $43</u>. You ask your broker to help you choose a Put to give you the opportunity to make a profit on the anticipated decline of the HD share price. Your broker tells you that the technical analysis shows that the price of HD could go below $38. Your broker advises you to buy 2 Put contracts with a <u>strike price of $40</u> which will <u>expire</u> on the third Friday of February. The <u>premium</u> for each share is $1.30; therefore, each contract (100 shares of HD) will cost $130 for a total of $260 for the 2 Put contracts (not including commissions). You decide to kick it up to 4 contacts for a total premium of $520. Your broker tells you that the contract month (February) has a code of HD-EU-E (the EU-E designates the contract series that has a strike price of $40 and expiration month of Feb) and this symbol allows you to follow what is happening to your contract pricing during the life of the 4 Put options.

In December, HD has some unexpected bad news and the stock plunges down to $36. You and your broker decide not to take profits yet (you make money with a Put when the price of the underlying stock goes down.). In January, the price has fallen to $32 and your HD-EU-E options are selling at a premium of $6 per share. You tell your broker to <u>close out your position</u>. You will have made a profit of $4.70 per share ($6–$1.30) for a total profit on the 4 put contracts (400 shares) of $1,880 for a whopping 361% return on the $520 premium you paid for the 4 Put contracts.

Buying a Put (long)

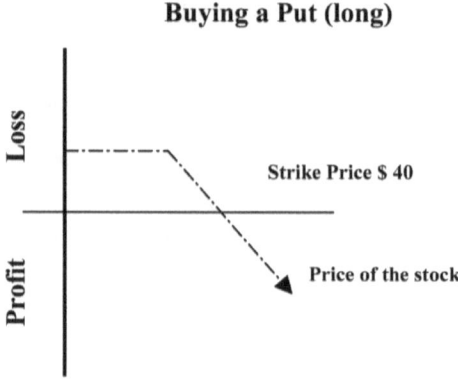

Fig. 2

To take profits or to cut losses, the contracts held must be "closed-out". In the case of a profit, the price at which the contract can be sold will be the price from which the original premium costs will be taken to make up the profit. (Don't forget commissions),

To cut losses before expiration, a contract can be sold (to close-out the position) and the price obtained will be subtracted from the original premium to figure the loss.

To sell or write an option contract is not the same thing as closing out a position, We will discuss writing a contract in the next section.

There are several <u>styles</u> of option contracts:

- American: The option can be exercised any time during the contract period.
- European: The option can only be exercised during a specific period.
- Capped: The option can only be exercised if it hits a "Cap Price".

As stated, this book is focused on the <u>American style</u>.

More important terminology:

<u>Intrinsic Value</u>: An option has two types of value: 1) Intrinsic value and 2) Time value. Intrinsic value is the difference between the stock price and the strike price, if that difference is a positive number. (Example: current price = $40 and strike price = $36, the Intrinsic value is $4). For <u>put options</u> it is also the difference between the strike price and the stock price, if that difference is positive. (Example: current price = $20 and strike price = $25; intrinsic value is $5).

<u>Time Value</u>: As an option gets closer to expiration it loses value because there is less time for price movement to happen. There may be a point—usually early in the option period that an option may have more value than just intrinsic value. This difference between intrinsic value and the total premium would be the time value.

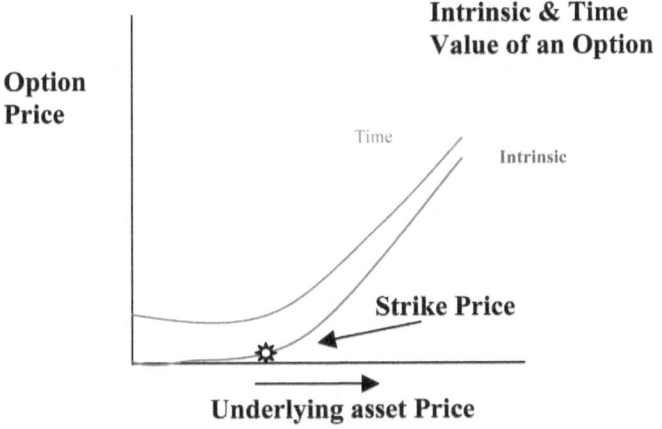

Fig. 3

Another way of explaining Intrinsic and Time value: If you purchase a call with a premium of $9, a strike price of $35 and the current stock price is $39.25. The option has $4.25 of intrinsic value and $4.75 of time value. Moreover, as the contract gets nearer expiration date, the Time value "decays" and moves toward zero

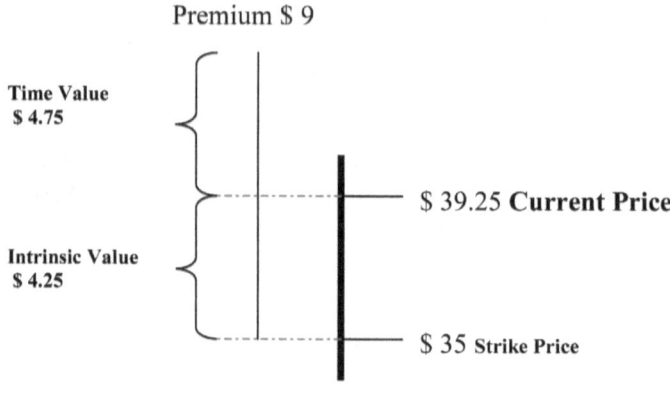

Fig. 4

In-the-money (ITM), Out-of-the-money (OTM) and At-the-Money (ATM)

- In-the-Money (ITM): When a <u>call</u> is purchased with a <u>strike price below the price of the underlying security</u>. This means that the option has <u>intrinsic value</u> and it is exercisable.

In the case of an in-the-money put, the strike price is above the price of the underlying security and thus has intrinsic value.

- Out-of-the-Money (OTM) is when a <u>call</u> is purchased with the <u>strike price above the current price of the underlying security</u>. The premium is totally made up of time value.

In the case of an out-of-the money <u>put, the strike price is below the current price of the underlying security</u>. The premium is made up of only time value.

- At-the-money (ATM) is when a call or put has <u>a strike price which is the same as the current price of the underlying security</u>. The option has no intrinsic value but may have time value (premium).

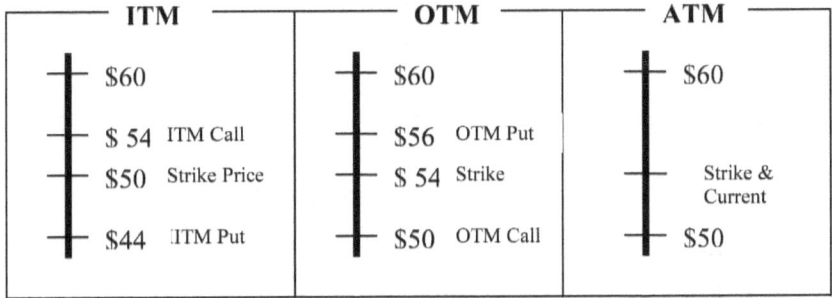

Fig. 5

As you saw in the examples of buying a call and buying a put, the option trader must not only work out the <u>direction</u> that the underlying stock might move but also <u>when</u> that movement might take place. <u>It's all about making money on movement—either up, down or no movement at all.</u>

Volatility

As stated previously, the game is all about prognosticating in which direction the underlying stock will move and when this movement might happen. When trading stock options, it is desirable to have an underlying stock that has a tendency to make large moves (more volatile) so that the derivative will also make larger move. This is a general statement because there are some traders that trade in options with low volatility and look for small gains that happen many times over. But for the most part, option traders like stocks with some volatility.

When we are looking for stocks with higher volatility, we can look for the stocks Beta. When a stock moves exactly in synch with the market, that stock is said to have a Beta of 1.0 when a stock moves in a more exaggerated manner than the overall market, it is said to have a Beta greater than 1.0. For example, if the market moves up 2% and a particular stock moves up 4% you could say that the stock has a Beta of 2.0. This is a simplification but you get the idea. A stocks Beta can be normally be found when looking up information on a stock. Conversely, when a stock is less volatile than the general market its' Beta will be below 1.0. By definition, as an option is a derivative of the underlying stock, there is a very strong correlation between the two and we can *assume* that a stock option will mirror the volatility of its underlying stock. Most traders want volatility.

Situational outcomes of option trading

A purchase of an option contract can have three possible outcomes:

1. The option (put or call) is in-the-money. In this case, the option holder can do several things: Close-out the position and take profits if it is near the profit goal; or hold the option and hope for the value of the option to increase before expiration of the period; or exercise the option to get an assignment of the underlying security at the strike price of the option.

2. The option (put or call) is out-of-the-money. In this case the holder can do several things: If the option is not moving as anticipated, the position can be closed-out and a loss taken which would be the difference between the purchase premium and the current premium at which the holder can sell the contract ("closing-out the position"). Or, the holder can not try to cut losses but hope that the option will move into the money before expiration. If nothing happens, the option expires and there is a total loss of the premium. <u>One of the "advantages" of losing money trading options is that you know what your maximum loss could be; whereas owning the underlying securities could pose large unknown losses</u>.

Who makes sure that option trading takes place in an orderly and responsible fashion?

In 1973, the Options Clearing Corporation (OCC) was founded and placed under the supervision of the Securities Exchange Commission (SEC). This private corporation is made up of qualified *Clearing Members* who are charged with the responsibility of making sure that all option transactions and responsibilities are met. The OCC derives its income from transaction fees.

The OCC operates an informative website at: www.optionsclearing.com

U.S Exchanges where options are traded

Listed options are traded on the following exchanges. The OCC does all the options clearing for all the listed exchanges below.

- American Stock Exchange
- Boston Stock Exchange
- Chicago Board of Options
- International Securities Exchange
- New York Stock Exchange, ARCA
- Philadelphia Stock Exchange

Covered Call

Up to now, we have only discussed the two most common and simplest positions. Let's review:

We know that when the trader believes that the underlying security will <u>move up</u> within a certain period of time, the trader will take a <u>long call position</u>. However, if the trader believes that the underlying security <u>will go down</u> in price within a certain period the trader will take a <u>long put position</u>.

Now we will talk about how to make money when we anticipate little or no movement in price of the underlying security.

<u>Covered call</u>: When a trader believes that there will be little movement in the underlying security (low Beta), one of the most conservative option trading strategies can be used—the covered call. This situation is a bit different in that the <u>trader owns shares of underlying security.</u> The trader believes that the underlying security will not have much movement and usually <u>writes an out-of-the-money call option</u> to sell to buyers who want to purchase calls on the underlying stock that the trader holds. The hope of the covered call writer is that the strike price will not be hit and the option will expire and the *writer* (as opposed to the *holder*) can <u>keep the premium from the sale of the options and also keep the underlying stock so that the process can be done again.</u> The goal is to make a series of smaller quick profits so as the total of these trades can produce an enviable annual return, which can compare favorably with the home run hitters.

If the writer is wrong and the option moves above the strike price, the underlying stock can be "called away" and the option to purchase the stock at the strike price must be honored and the *writer* must present his stock for assignment to the *holder*. In which case, the writer keeps the premium and is paid the strike price for the called away stock. Covered calls are considered conservative in that if nothing unforeseen happens to the underlying stock, the worst case scenario is that the stock is called away and the writer may lose only the potential future gains or dividends of the stock.

Example: The trader owns 500 shares of Home Depot (HD). The trader feels that HD is a long term hold and the owner may have already made money on the stock's appreciation. HD has been stuck within a range of $38–$43 and the current price is $39.25; there has been little movement in the stock and the trader looks for some income from his listless stock.

The trader checks the quotes for call options for HD and notices that HD May options (HD EV-E) have a current premium of $4.25 per share with a strike price of $42.50. The trader does the math and sees that the 500 shares he would use to "cover" the sale of the 5 call contracts (500 shares) would total $2,125. He calls his broker and finds out what commissions there would be to write 5 call contracts. He then writes the five contracts and an option trader purchases the contracts. The *writer* receives the premiums for the five contracts. If the HD-EV-E contracts don't hit the strike price of $42.50 the *writer* keeps the premiums and the stock. He has two months until the third Friday of May so he hopes that HD won't hit the strike price and the options will expire. As good fortune would have it, May comes and goes and the trader has made a 10.8% return on the value of his underlying stock. The trader is happy and decides to do it again and starts looking for another attractive premium opportunity.

But there's more ...

Making profits on the sale of underlying stock with an ITM call

Suppose the owner of 500 shares of HD wants to sell the shares ... Instead of calling his/her broker and telling the broker to sell the shares, the owner can write an in-the-money call. Keep in mind that ITM calls have higher premiums because of intrinsic and time value.

Example: The owner of the shares sees that an in-the-money call costs a premium of $9 per share for an HD-EG-E (May contract month with a strike price of $35, which is in the money because the current price of HD is $39.25). For the five contracts (500 shares), the owner would get a premium of $4500 less commissions for writing ITM options for the 500 shares he/she owns. The stock price is currently $39.25 and the calls will probably be exercised and the 500 shares will have to be assigned for the strike price of $35, and, therefore, the owner will lose $4.25 per share ($39.25–$35) for a loss of $2125. But the difference between the premiums ($4500) for the ITM covered calls and the projected loss of $2125 still gives the owner a net profit of $2375 and would give the owner a 12.1% return on the sale of the underlying stock instead of selling at the current market price of $39.25 and paying commissions to sell the stock. What makes this covered call attractive is the time value of the option.

Below is an illustration of the option values of the ITM covered call from the above example

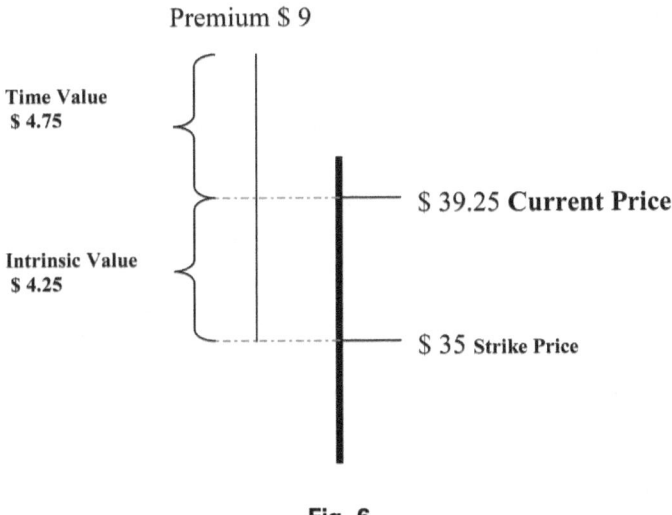

Fig. 6

If you have understood what you have read so far, then you are probably asking yourself: "is a covered put the same as a covered call—only in reverse?" The answer is yes and no. There are some peculiarities with "shorting a stock" which make the covered put a little different and for the time being let's leave that discussion for another time.

So far, you have learned how options can make money when the underlying stock can go up (call), down (put) and neutral (covered call). These option trading techniques are considered the most straight forward and easy to understand strategies. It is important for the new trader to understand how these work. If you don't have a good feel about how basic option strategies work, go back and review and follow the examples carefully.

Underlying stock trend	Up	Neutral	Down
Option	Call	Covered Call	Put

Fig.7   Basic trading Strategies

To repeat: the game is to analyze the direction of the price movements of the underlying security and when the movements might take place. Yes, indeed, the devil is in the details when trying to figure out these key questions and we will discuss that subject in great detail in the next chapter.

A brief introduction to complex option strategies

You have been introduced to the two most basic and common trading strategies—the put, call and covered call. But experienced traders use many combinations of Long (buy) and Short (selling) positions to take advantage of movement trends and at the same time reduce (hedge) risk. The purpose of introducing these positions is to give you a glimpse of what may lay ahead after the new trader gains experience and confidence in using the simple long call, long put or covered call stock option trading strategies.

Spreads

A spread is when a trader is both buyer and seller (writer) of the same type of option (call or put) on the same underlying security with different strike prices and or expiration dates.

- Bull spread: Long a call with a low strike price and short a call with a higher strike price, or long a put with a low strike price and short a put with a higher strike price.
- Bear spread: Short a call with a low exercise price and long a call with a higher exercise price, or short a put with a low exercise price and long a put with a higher exercise price.
- Box Spread: Any combination of options that has a constant payoff at expiration. For example combining a long butterfly made with calls, with a short butterfly made with puts will have a constant payoff of zero, and in equilibrium will cost zero. In practice any profit from these spreads can be eaten up by commissions (hence the name "alligator spreads").

Straddle

Long a call and long a put with the same exercise prices (a long straddle), or short a call and short a put with the same exercise prices (a short straddle).

Strangle

Long a call and long a put with different strike prices (a long strangle), or short a call and short a put with different strike prices (a short strangle).

Butterflies

Butterflies require trading options with 3 different exercise prices. Assume exercise prices $X1 < X2 < X3$ and that $(X1 + X3)/2 = X2$

- Long butterfly—long 1 call with exercise price X1, short 2 calls with exercise price X2, and long 1 call with exercise price X3. Alternatively, long 1 put with exercise price X1, short 2 puts with exercise price X2, and long 1 put with exercise price X3.
- Short butterfly—short 1 call with exercise price X1, long 2 calls with exercise price X2, and short 1 call with exercise price X3. Alternatively, short 1 put with exercise price X1, long 2 puts with exercise price X2, and short 1 put with exercise price X3.

These more exotic positions will be covered in detail in the sequel to this book. It's recommended that until some experience is obtained with the simple long call, long put and covered call positions, the new trader hold off using the more complex positions.

Other Types of Options:

Index Options

Like an option based on an underling security, Index options allow the trader to derive an option from a spectrum of individual stocks classified and grouped by sectors, capitalization and other identifiable qualities. There are more than 40 different indices. Each index is made up of a weighted sampling of the particular market and this sampling is the underlying asset which defines the option. Like a mutual fund, the diversity of the components of the index provides for less volatility than the single equity option. These indexes allow traders to speculate on narrow and broad markets and function just as options derived from individual securities. Examples of the smorgasbord of indices traded can be found at the following links:

http://www.cboe.com/LearnCenter/workbench/products/sp100.htm
http://www.cboe.com/LearnCenter/workbench/products/russell.htm
http://www.cboe.com/LearnCenter/workbench/products/nasdaq.htm
http://www.cboe.com/LearnCenter/workbench/products/dow.htm
http://www.cboe.com/LearnCenter/workbench/volatility/intro.htm

LEAPS[2]

Long-Term Equity Anticipation Securities (LEAPS) are long-term options available on over 300 equities and 11 indices. LEAPS provide traders and investors with a longer-term view (some with a period of several years) of the market as a whole or on an individual stock. As with traditional short-term options, LEAPS are available in two types, calls and puts.

As you can probably anticipate, because of the time value of longer periods, LEAP premiums are more expensive than normal option premiums

---

2   Chicago Board of Options Exchange(CBOE)

Equity LEAPS Benefits

- Equity LEAPS calls can provide long-term stock market investors an opportunity to benefit from the growth of large capitalization companies (expensive) without having to make an outright stock purchases.
- Equity LEAPS puts can provide a hedge for stock investors against substantial declines in the underlying equities.
- Current equity options users may also find LEAPS appealing if they desire to take a longer term position of up to three years in some of the same options they currently trade.

Index LEAPS Benefits

- Index LEAPS let you trade, hedge or invest in the "entire" stock market or select industry sectors for a time that can be measured in years.
- Index options let you take a bullish or bearish position on the entire market. Index options let you hedge your investments against adverse market moves.
- Index LEAPS let you do all this over a longer time period.

Some major factors affecting option prices (premiums):

- The underlying stock price in relation to the strike price (*intrinsic value*)
- The quality of the underlying stock
- The length of time until the option expires (*time value*)
- How much the price fluctuates (*volatility value*)?
- Fundamental economic issues of the economy in general
- Fundamental financial and political issues of the underlying stock
- Technical indicators.
- Supply and demand for options involving the underlying stock

Commissions

Commissions depend on whether you have an online or full service account. Average online trading accounts charge about $10 per trade plus a charge of about $1 per contract. A full service account can be around $18 per trade plus $1.50 per contract. Regardless, commissions need to be taken into account to figure the actual break—even for a trade.

Example: You purchase 5 calls using your online account. The commissions would be $15. If you purchase the 5 contracts for a premium of $3 each share for a cost of $1500 plus $15 for a total of $1515. As a result, the break even is $3.03.

How to read a stock option quote

The table below is an example of a quote for Home Depot for the Calls and Puts for May 2007. The current price of the underlying HD stock was $41.25. There are many different ways that quotes can be presented, but the below is typical. Note the ITM premiums as opposed to the OTM strike prices for both Calls and Puts.

Put	Last	Bid	Ask	Change	Open Int	Vol	Strike Price
.HDQE	0.05	0.00	0.05	0.0	503	0	25.0
.HDQY	0.03	0.00	0.05	0.0	284	0	27.5
.HDQF	0.15	0.05	0.10	0.0	1120	0	30.0
.HDQZ	0.25	0.20	0.25	0.0	11065	0	32.5
.HDQG	0.50	0.45	0.50	0.0	8446	0	35.0
.HDQU	1.00	1.00	1.05	-0.1	22433	0	37.5
.HDQH	1.95	1.90	2.00	0.0	7175	0	40.0
1	2	3	4	5	6	7	8

1. symbol for the month and strike price
2. Price of the last contract sale
3. Price the buyer is offering
4. Price the seller is asking
5. Percent change
6. Number of contracts open
7. Volume of options contracts sold today
8. Strike Price—Price at which the option can be exercised

Call	Last	Bid	Ask	Change	Open Int	Vol	Strike Price
.HDEE	14.40	15.30	15.60	0.0	583	0	25.0
.HDEY	11.90	12.90	13.10	0.0	280	0	27.5
.HDEF	10.40	10.50	10.70	0.0	549	0	30.0
.HDEZ	8.30	8.20	8.40	0.0	360	0	32.5
.HDEG	6.10	6.00	6.20	0.0	1552	0	35.0
.HDEU	4.20	4.10	4.30	0.0	10540	0	37.5
.HDES	0.33	0.30	0.35	0.0	1329	0	40.0
1	2	3	4	5	6	7	8

Fig. 8

Besides price, one of the most important quote elements is open interest; it shows the amount of liquidity and when the number starts to diminish it shows that traders are closing-out their positions.

Advantages of Trading Stock and Index Options

- Leverage: Options allow a relatively small amount of money to control a much larger value of an underlying asset.
- Profits can be generated on up, down and sideways movement of an underlying asset.
- Options can be derived from assets as narrow as an individual company or as broad as entire markets.
- Hedging: Options can be used to offset a position to protect against contrary moves in the underlying asset
- Options can be used to reduce commissions or actually make additional profits on the sale of stock.
- Options have a fixed amount of maximum loss.
- There are other advantages and these will be discussed in the next sequel, "Advanced Option Trading"

Summary of Chapter 1

- A *Trader* is defined as someone who regularly buys something and sells it for a profit within a short period of time. An *Investor* purchases something with the purpose of reselling at a profit after a longer period of time as compared to a *trader.*

- A stock option trader (speculator) not only must analyze the direction of price movement of a security but also the time when movement might occur.

- Profits can be generated on up, down and no movement of an underlying asset.

- An option is also called a *derivative* in that it derives its value from an underlying asset.

- The purchase of a <u>Call</u> contract conveys the right—but not the obligation—to <u>buy</u> 100 shares of an underlying asset at a specific price anytime before the expiration of the contract period.

- The purchase of a <u>Put</u> contract conveys the right—but not the obligation—to <u>sell</u> 100 shares of an underlying asset at a specific price anytime before the expiration of the contract period.

- In-the-Money (ITM): When a call is purchased with a strike price below the current price of the underlying security.

- Out-of-the-Money (OTM) is when a call is purchased with the strike price above the current price of the underlying security.

- A Covered Call can be used when movement is thought to be static.

- Complex Positions: Spread, Straddles, Butterflies, etc. It's recommended that until some experience is obtained with the simple long call, long put and covered call positions, the new trader hold off on the more complex positions

- Index options allow traders to speculate on narrow and broad markets and the underlying asset is a selection of weighted securities within the asset or market group. Because of the diversification, Index options are usually less volatile than individual equity options.

- Basic Trading Strategies

Underlying stock direction	Up	Neutral	Down
Option	Call	Covered Call	Put

- LEAPS: Long-Term Equity Anticipation Securities are long term options.
- An Option has two types of value: Intrinsic and Time

Some major factors affecting option prices (premiums):

- The underlying stock price in relation to the strike price (*intrinsic value*)
- The quality of the underlying stock
- The length of time until the option expires (*time value*)
- How much the price fluctuates (*volatility value*).
- Fundamental economic issues of the economy in general
- Fundamental financial and political issues of the underlying stock
- Technical indicators.
- Supply and demand for options involving the underlying stock

We have casually talked about the most difficult part of trading options: how does a trader ascertain what direction the underlying stock or index price will move and when might that happen? That's the simple nitty-gritty. If you can do both of those things, your financial worries are over. Drinks are on you! But as you will see in the next chapter, there is no free lunch and sweat and tears are still part of making "easy money".

CHAPTER 2

Fundamental and Technical Analysis

In the last chapter, we noted that the key to successful trading was in proper anticipation of the direction of price movement and the period in which that movement might happen. This chapter will introduce some of the more basic and most used methods to help analyze potential performance of an underlying stock, which will most likely describe the movement of the derivative option.

There are two main schools of the philosophy of analysis of equities: *Fundamental and Technical.* These two philosophies are not mutually exclusive and may be used together to help the trader drive a successful trade. These approaches are not natural laws of nature and they are in a state of endless "tweaking" as each trader hunts for a "secret formula for success", which is usually guarded as closely as a secret love affair with a close relative. Many books and articles have been written on both approaches, but the fact that both are based on past history, underscores that there is no guarantee that history will repeat itself; therein lays the risk to all investors and traders for <u>the future is nothing but a probability.</u>

"Never try to time the market" is one of those clichés one constantly hears but in the world of trading options, it's all about timing.

Fundamental Analysis

Fundamentalists look mostly at the financial information about the company, which is similar to a doctor reviewing a blood test. The company might look healthy on the outside but its financial numbers may reveal something else. Fundamentalists also like to look at the "story" surrounding the company: is there a new product coming out which will knock the socks off the competitors?; is the SEC about to investigate the company?; has the company just entered into a risky strategy?, what affects will a corporate restructuring have on the company?, etc. A fundamentalist will throw all of these factors into the mix and subjectively weigh the risk-reward.

Because the fundamentalist philosophy is probably more appropriate for *investing* (long term), we will not go into great detail but touch upon some of the important sources of financial information that even an option trader should understand.

The Balance Sheet

The Balance Sheet is a financial statement that summarizes a company's assets, liabilities and shareholders' equity on a particular day. These three elements of a balance sheet can give investors an idea as to what the company owns and owes, as well as the amount invested by the shareholders and how well the management of the company is using assets and managing its debt.

The balance sheet is divided into two parts that, based on the following equation, must equal (or balance out) each other. The main formula behind a balance sheet is: assets = liabilities + shareholders' equity.

Balance Sheet for Wal-Mart			
As of Jan 31, 2006			
Assets		**Liabilities and Shareholders' Equity**	
Current Assets:		*Current Liabilities:*	
Cash and Cash Equivalents	6,414	Commercial Paper	3,754
Receivables	2,662	Accounts Payable	25,373
Inventories	32,191	Accrued Liabilities	13,465
Prepaid Expenses and Other	2,557	Accrued Income Taxes	1,340
Total Current Assets	43,824	Long-term Debt, due within one year	4,595
		Obligations Under Capital Leases, due within one year	299
Property and Equipment, at cost:		**Total Current Liabilities**	48,826
Land	16,643		
Buildings and Improvements	56,163	Long-term Debt	26,429
Fixtures and Equipment	22,750	Long-term Obligations Under Capital Leases	3,742
Transportation Equipment	1,746	Deferred Income Taxes and Other	4,552
Total Property and Equipment, at cost:	97,302	Minority Interest	1,467
Less Accumulated Depreciation	21,427		
Property and Equipment, net	75,875	*Shareholders' Equity:*	
		Preferred Stock	0
Property Under Capital Lease:	5,578	Common Stock	417
Less Accumulated Amortization	2,163	Capital in Excess of Par Value	2,596
		Accumulated Other Comprehensive Income	1,053
Property Under Capital Lease, net	3,415	Retained Earnings	49,105
Goodwill	12,188		
Other Assets and Deferred Charges	2,885	**Total Shareholders' Equity**	53,171
Total Assets	138,187	**Total Liabilities and Shareholders' Equity**	138,187

Fig.10

Financial ratio analysis uses formulas to gain insight into the company and its operations. For the balance sheet, using financial ratios (like the <u>debt-to-equity ratio</u>) can show you a better idea of the company's financial condition along with its operational efficiency. It is important to note that some ratios will need information from more than one financial statement, such as from the balance sheet and the income statement.

The main types of ratios that use information from the balance sheet are financial strength ratios and activity ratios. Financial strength ratios, such as the <u>working capital</u> and debt-to-equity ratios, provide information on how well the company can meet its obligations and how they are leveraged. This can give investors an idea of how financially stable the company is and how the company finances itself. Activity ratios focus mainly on current accounts to show how well the company manages its operating cycle (which include receivables, inventory and payables). These ratios can provide insight into the operational efficiency of the company.[3] There are a wide range of individual financial ratios that investors use to learn more about a company.

<u>The current ratio</u> is used to test the short-term liability-paying ability of a business. It's calculated by dividing total current assets by total current liabilities in a company's most recent balance sheet. From the data in the example below:

The total current assets of $43,824 (millions) divided by the total current liabilities of $48,826 equals a Current Ratio of: 9[4]. This means that the company has 90 cents of current assets (can be turned into cash within 12 months) to cover $1 of debt due within 12 months. As a general rule, a company with a Current Ratio of 2.0 or more is considered in good financial position to meet its short term obligations.

---

3   accountinginfo.com

4   Wal-Mart is a little different in that much of its inventory is not owned. Wal-Mart leases-out its shelf space to vendors. Normally, a company owns its inventory which would raise the ratio considerably.

Balance Sheet for Wal-Mart			
As of Jan 31, 2006			
Assets		**Liabilities and Shareholders' Equity**	
Current Assets:		*Current Liabilities:*	
Cash and Cash Equivalents	6,414	Commercial Paper	3,754
Receivables	2,662	Accounts Payable	25,373
Inventories	32,191	Accrued Liabilities	13,465
Prepaid Expenses and Other	2,557	Accrued Income Taxes	1,340
Total Current Assets	43,824	Long-term Debt, due within one year	4,595
		Obligations Under Capital Leases, due within one year	299
Property and Equipment, at cost:		**Total Current Liabilities**	48,826
Land	16,643		
Buildings and Improvements	56,163	Long-term Debt	26,429
Fixtures and Equipment	22,750	Long-term Obligations Under Capital Leases	3,742
Transportation Equipment	1,746	Deferred Income Taxes and Other	4,552
Total Property and Equipment, at cost:	97,302	Minority Interest	1,467
Less Accumulated Depreciation	21,427		
Property and Equipment, net	75,875	*Shareholders' Equity:*	
		Preferred Stock	0
Property Under Capital Lease:	5,578	Common Stock	417
Less Accumulated Amortization	2,163	Capital in Excess of Par Value	2,596
		Accumulated Other Comprehensive Income	1,053
Property Under Capital Lease, net	3,415	Retained Earnings	49,105
Goodwill	12,188		
Other Assets and Deferred Charges	2,885	**Total Shareholders' Equity**	53,171
Total Assets	138,187	**Total Liabilities and Shareholders' Equity**	138,187

Fig. 11   Balance Sheet

A more severe measure of the short-term liability-paying ability of a business is the acid test ("Quick") ratio, which excludes inventory (and prepaid expenses also). Only cash, market-able securities investments (if any), and accounts receivable are counted as sources to pay the current liabilities of the business. It is also called the quick ratio because only cash and assets quickly convertible into cash are included in the amount available for paying current liabilities. *The rule of thumb is that a company's acid test ratio should be 1 to 1 or better,* although you find many more exceptions to this as compared with the 2 to 1 current ratio standard.

The Operating Statement[5]

The income statement is the most popular financial statement in an annual or quarterly Company report required to be filed by the SEC. The income statement is the "sexy" portion of the financial statements because it includes figures such as revenue, net income and earnings per share (EPS). In essence, an income statement tells you how much revenue a company produced and the profits made after all expenses, which are clearly described in the income statement (also called the operating Statement). The income statement is simply designed, and is even simpler to read. The statement is

---

5   Investopedia.com

looked at from top to bottom. The top line lists the revenue (sales) brought in. Each subsequent line deducts expenses and costs from the revenue figure until you finally get to the bottom line (net income). Each item that has a line above the number means that it is a subtotal or total (the net income usually has a bold or double line below the number). Below is the typical layout of an income statement. There isn't one cookie-cutter way to present a company's income statement. The exact information presented depends, to some extent, on the type of business the company operates. On the next page is an example:

YEARS ENDED	1999	1998
NET SALES	$12,154	$8,488
Cost of sales	4,240	2,924
Gross margin	7,914	5,564
Expenses:		
Research and development	1,594	1,026
Sales and marketing	2,447	1,572
General and administrative	418	262
Purchased research and development	471	594
Total operating expenses	4,930	3,454
OPERATIING INCOME	2,984	2,110
Realized gains on sale of investment		5
Interest and other income, net	332	196
Income before provision for income taxes	3,316	2,311
Provision for income taxes	1,220	956
NET INCOME	$ 2,096	$1,355
Net income per common share—basic	$ 0.65	$ 0.44
Net income per common share—diluted	$ 0.62	$ 0.42
Shares used in per-share calculation—basic	3,213	3,094
Shares used in per-share calculation—diluted	3,398	3,245

Fig. 12   The Operating (Income) Statement

Earnings per share (EPS)

One of the most-used ratios in stock value and securities analysis is earnings per share (EPS). The essential calculation of earnings per share is as follows:

Net Income Available for Common Stockholders/Total Number of Outstanding Common Stock Shares = basic earnings per hare

Price-Earnings ratio (P/E)

The market price of stock shares of a public company corporation is compared with its basic EPS and expressed in the price/earnings ratio (P/E) as follows:

Current Market Price of Stock Shares/Basic Earnings per Share = Price/Earnings Ratio

How to estimate the future value of stock shares using P/E Multiple

A P/E multiple can be used to forecast a future value of a stock. Let's say a company has a current stock price of $30 and earned $2 per share. If an analyst comes out with a forecast for next year for earnings of $4 per share, we can use the current P/E ratio of 15 and forecast a future stock price of $60 ($4 per share estimated earnings x 15 P/E ratio).

Return on Investment (ROI) or Return on Equity (ROE)

Owners take the risk of whether their business can earn a profit and sustain its profit performance over the years. How much would you pay for a business that consistently suffers a loss? The value of the owners' investment depends first and foremost on the past and future profit performance of the business relative to the capital invested to earn that profit.

For instance, suppose a business earns $100,000 annual net income for its stockholders. If its stockholders' equity is only $250,000, then its profit performance relative to the stockholders' capital used to make that profit is 40%, which is very good indeed. If, on the other hand, stockholders' equity is 10 times as much ($2,500,000) then the company's profit performance is 4%, which is terrible relative to the owners' capital tied up in the business to earn that profit. It would be better to purchase government bonds with no risk!

The point is that profit should be compared with the amount of capital invested to earn that profit. Profit for a period divided by the amount of capital invested to earn that profit is called return on investment, or ROI for short. ROI is a broad concept that applies to almost any sort of investment of capital. The owners' investment in a business is the total of the owners' equity accounts in the company's balance sheet.

Dividing annual net income by stockholders' equity gives the return on equity ratio (ROE). ROE should be compared with industry-wide averages and with investment alternatives.

Quarterly and Annual Reports

We find most historical data in the annual and quarterly reports released by a company's management. These can be found over the internet or in physical form.

Financial statements are required by law and must include a balance sheet, an income statement, a statement of cash flows, an auditor's report and a relatively detailed description of the company's operations and prospects for the upcoming year.

The annual report is sometimes also referred to as the 10-K, but don't be fooled. The 10-K contains the same information but in much more detail than many annual reports.

The following information is presented in most financial reports, note that the order in which these are presented might vary:

- Summary of the previous year
- Information about the company in general—its history, products and line of business
- Letter to shareholders from the president or the CEO
- Auditor's report detailing the accuracy of the results

Where to find company reports

Thanks to the Internet, finding financial reports is easier than ever. Nowadays, every reputable company has an investor relations section on its website that is a wealth of information.

If you want to dig deeper and go beyond the slick marketing version of the annual report found on corporate websites, you'll have to search through filings made to the Securities and Exchange Commission (SEC). All publicly-traded companies in the U.S. must file regular financial reports with the SEC. These filings include the annual report (known as the 10-K), quarterly report (10-Q) and a myriad of other forms containing all types of financial data.

Reports are filed through a system known as EDGAR (Electronic Data Gathering, Analysis and Retrieval system). EDGAR performs automated collection, validation, indexing, acceptance and forwarding of submissions by companies and others required by law to file forms with the SEC. Information on EDGAR can be found on the SEC's website, where you can search through forms as well as familiarize yourself with the system using its *EDGAR tutorial.*

Fundamental analysis boils down to: if the company has good ratios and a good story the price of the stock will most probably go up over time if the underlying market is also moving up. On the flip side, anyone looking for a stock to "short" would turn the good ratios and good story upside down: a company with ratios below standards and with a gloomy story will probably have declining stock price over time particularly in a declining market.

But fundamental analysis does little to address the problem of when an anticipated price movement might happen. This fact tends to make fundamentalists investors and not traders. Traders normally find technical analysis more appropriate to their objectives of determining what direction and when a stock price might move.

Technical Analysis

The central idea of technical analysis is that all of the numerous factors that investors and traders take into consideration about a company are reflected in the price of the stock and other measurable parameters. The thousands or millions of investors/traders that drive the market reach a sort of consensus symbolized by price and other transaction related variables of a company's stock. A trader or investor who practices technical analysis read the "tea leaves" of quantifiable historical performance.

Charting

Technical analysis takes full advantage of the fact that a "picture is worth a thousand words". The basic way to depict the daily price movement of a particular asset is depicted as a bar which will demonstrate the daily high, low and close for the stock .

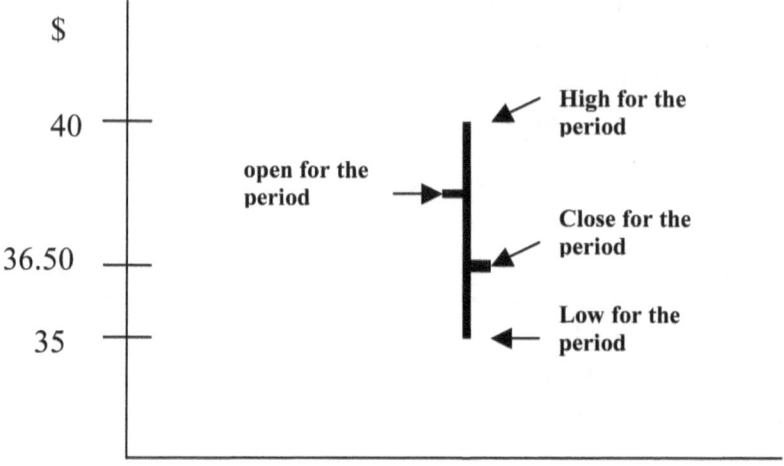

Fig. 13   Price Bar

Charts can be of various durations: hourly, daily, monthly, yearly, etc. Below are three different time periods for Microsoft: The top is the weekly; middle is the weekly and the bottom is the yearly chart.

Daily

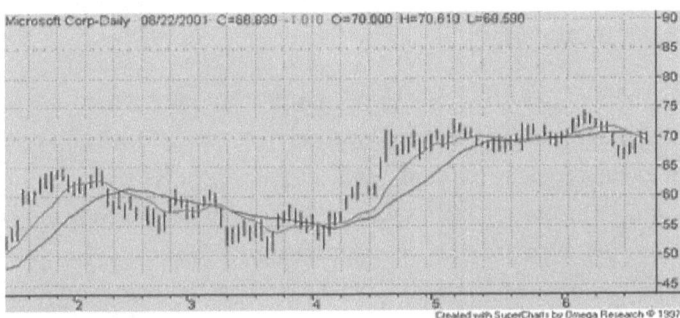

Weekly

Yearly

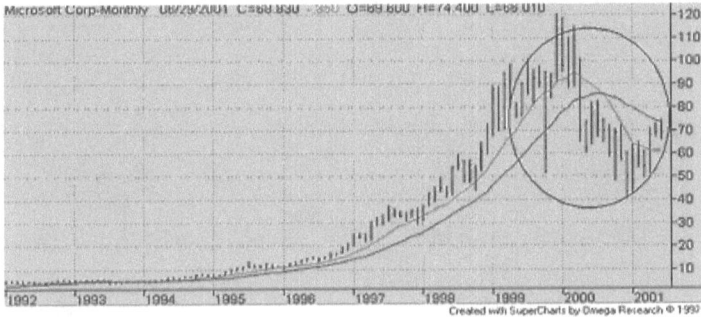

Fig. 14

The red and blue lines are called moving averages which we will talk about in detail. But as you can see, it is fairly easy to see trends in the price movement of the stock. Learning to read these patterns of movement is vital to helping the trader pick <u>entry and exit points</u>, estimate which <u>direction</u> the stock will move, when a change in direction might take place and where a possible move might find <u>support</u> or <u>resistance</u>.

Charts also help to identify repetitive patterns of movement which can act as high probability indicators. Moreover, charts can graphically display when certain key events took place and what impact they had on the price of the stock (this is a point where fundamental and technical analysis may coincide). But before you get overloaded with information, let's use an example one way a chart alone might be used to predict when and in what direction an underlying stock might move.

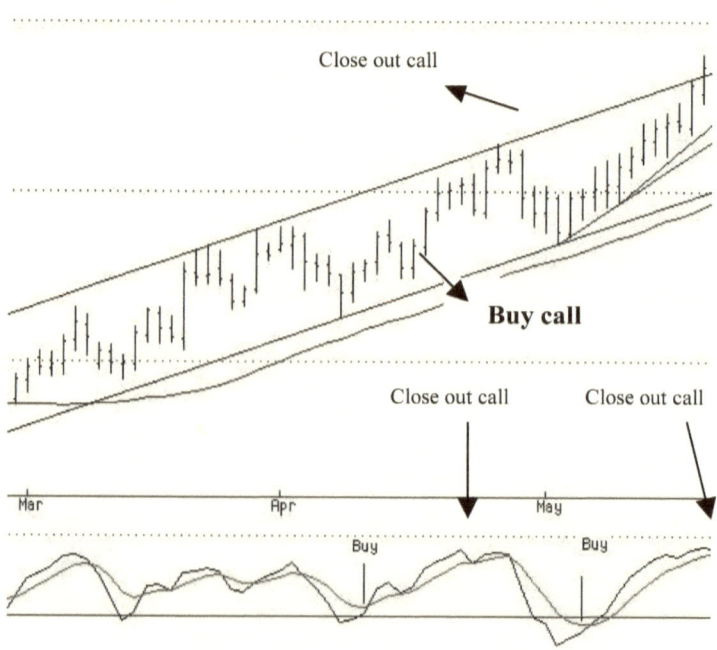

Fig. 15   Channel Analysis

In this example, the bar chart above the line chart identifies a "channel" for a specific time period by placing a boundary line where the various highs and lows occur. Notice that over the "longer view", the highs become higher and the lows become higher. This demonstrates an up trend even though during shorter intervals, the price movement looks like a roller coaster. The upper channel line shows areas of resistance and the lower channel line shows area of support. As the shorter term price cycles snake up the channel, a trader will note how the price reacts as it hits either resistance of support. If a trader wants to make money on a chart like this one, there are two preferred <u>entry points</u> 1) to make money on upward movement, the trader would buy a call at on of the low points and plan to <u>close-out</u> the call when the price moves to the top of the cycle or; 2) buy a put at the top of the cycle and close out as the price nears the bottom of the channel. Because options usually cover a period of five months or—in the case of LEAPS—up to several years, it is best to choose a chart period which will give the best view of the length of time the trader wishes to use. Channel analysis is the most basic use of a price bar chart to try to <u>predict</u> when and in what direction price will move within a certain time period. Yes, the charts are based on history, but it is a matter of probability that something will happen to make the cyclical patterns deviate from the current trend. That is why a trader must be ready to take a loss from time to time but believe that the momentum and direction of the underlying asset will—most of the time—follow a predictable pattern. If a trader can "ride the wave" of a cycle over numerous trades the trader will come out a winner.

Moving Averages

Don't freak out when we start doing some math. There are fantastic computer programs and online stock screens that do all the number crunching for you but it is important to understand the principles involved in producing the charts that are basic the tools of the trade.

A chart of a Moving Average is another way to picture what shorter term cycles are doing within a larger cycle. As in channel analysis, after we note the overall trend of the price movement we try to locate supporting trends which work within the long trend.

What is a moving average? Moving averages are used to smooth out short-term fluctuations, which make it easier to identify trends or cycles. There are several variations of the moving average concept so we will begin with the simple moving average.

Simple moving average (SMA) [6]

The following examples are from StockCharts.com a provider of professionally produced charting and technical analysis.

A simple moving average is formed by computing the average (mean) price of a security over a specified number of periods. While it is possible to create moving averages from the Open, the High, and the Low data points, most moving averages are created using the closing price. For example: a 5-day simple moving average is calculated by adding the closing prices for the last 5 days and dividing the total by 5.

$$10 + 11 + 12 + 13 + 14 = 60$$

$$60 \div 5 = 12$$

The calculation is repeated for each price bar on the chart. The averages are then joined to form a smooth curving line—the **moving** average line. Continuing our example, if the next closing price in the average is 15, then this new period would be added and the oldest day, which is 10, would be dropped. The new 5-day simple moving average would be calculated as follows:

$$11 + 12 + 13 + 14 + 15 = 65$$

$$65 \div 5 = 13$$

Over the last 2 days, the SMA moved from 12 to 13. As new days are added, the old days will be subtracted and the moving average will continue to move over time.

---

6   Investopedia.com

Day	Daily Close	10-day SMA
1	67.50	
2	66.50	
3	66.44	
4	66.44	
5	66.25	
6	65.88	
7	66.63	
8	66.56	
9	65.63	
10	66.06	66.39
11	63.94	66.03
12	64.13	65.79
13	64.50	65.60
14	62.81	65.24
15	61.88	64.80
16	62.50	64.46
17	61.44	63.94
18	60.13	63.30
19	61.31	62.87
20	61.38	62.40

Fig. 16

In the example above, using closing prices from Eastman Kodak (EK), day 10 is the first day possible to calculate a 10-day simple moving average. As the calculation continues, the newest day is added and the oldest day is subtracted. The 10-day SMA for day 11 is calculated by adding the prices of day 2 through day 11 and dividing by 10. The averaging process then moves on to the next day where the 10-day SMA for day 12 is calculated by adding the prices of day 3 through day 12 and dividing by 10.

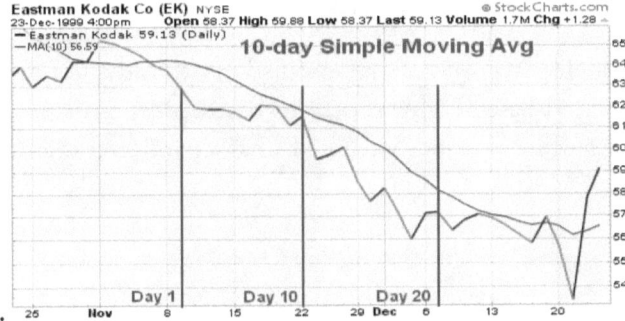

Fig.17

The chart above is a plot that contains the data sequence in the table. The simple moving average begins on day 10 and continues.

This simple illustration highlights the fact that all moving averages are lagging indicators and will always be "behind" the price. The price of EK is trending down, but the simple moving average, which is based on the previous 10 days of data, remains above the price. If the price were rising, the SMA would most likely be below. Because moving averages are lagging indicators, they fit in the category of trend following indicators. When prices are trending, moving averages work well. However, when prices are not trending, moving averages can give misleading signals

Exponential Moving Average (EMA)

In order to reduce the lag in simple moving averages, technicians often use exponential moving averages (also called exponentially weighted moving averages). EMA's reduce the lag by applying more weight to recent prices relative to older prices. The weighting applied to the most recent price depends on the specified period of the moving average. The shorter the EMA's period, the more weight to be applied to the most recent price. For example: a 10-period exponential moving average weighs the most recent price 18.18% while a 20-period EMA weighs the most recent price 9.52%. As we'll see, the calculating and EMA is much harder than calculating an SMA. The important thing to remember is that the exponential moving average puts more weight on recent prices. As such, it will react quicker to recent price changes than a simple moving average. Here's the calculation formula.

Exponential Moving Averages can be specified in two ways—as a percent-based EMA or as a period-based EMA. A percent-based EMA has a percentage as its single parameter while a period-based EMA has a parameter that represents the duration of the EMA.

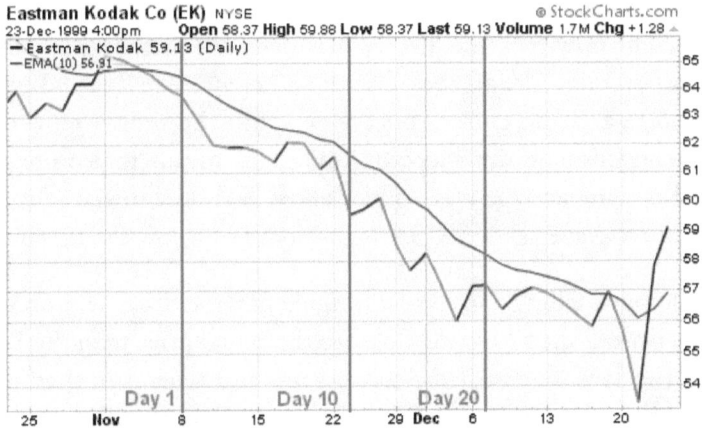

Fig. 18

Simple Versus Exponential

From afar, it would appear that the difference between an exponential moving average and a simple moving average is minimal. The exponential moving average is consistently closer to the actual price. On average, the EMA is 3/8 of a point closer to the actual price than the SMA.

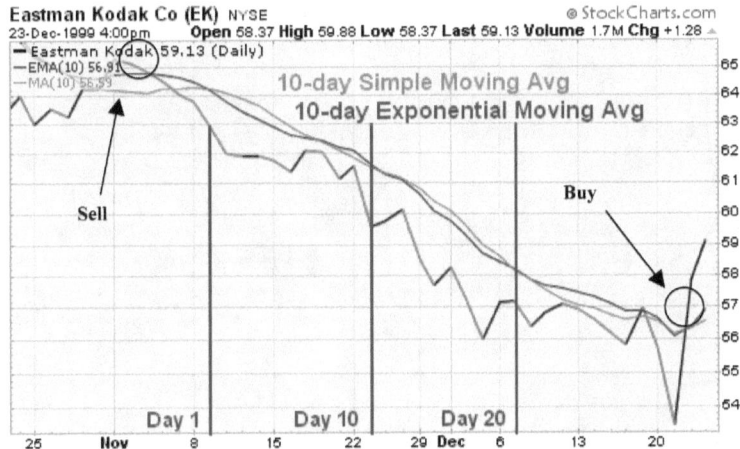

Fig. 19

From day 10 to day 20, the EMA was closer to the price than the SMA 9 out of 10 times. The only time the SMA was closer was in period number 18, and this did not last long. The average absolute difference between the exponential moving average and the current price was 1 and the simple moving average had an average absolute difference of 1.33. This means that on average, the exponential moving average was 1 point above or below the current price and the simple moving average was 1.33 points above or below the current price.

When EK stopped falling and started to trade flat, the SMA kept on declining. During this period, the SMA was closer to the actual price than the EMA. The EMA began to level out with the actual price and remain further away. This was because the actual price started to level out. Because of its lag, the SMA continued to decline and even touched the actual price on Dec 13th.

A comparison of a 50-day EMA and a 50-day SMA for IBM also shows that the EMA picks up on the trend quicker than the SMA. The blue arrows mark points when the stock started a strong trend. By giving more weight to recent prices, the EMA reacted quicker than the SMA and remained closer to the actual price.

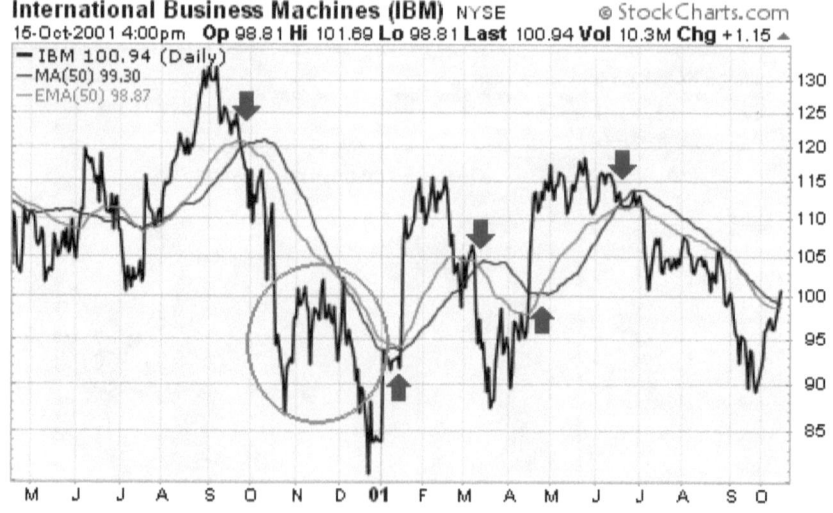

Fig. 20

The gray circle shows when the trend began to slow and a trading range developed. When the change from trend to trading began, the SMA was closer to the price. As the trading range continued into 2001, both moving averages converged. In early 2001, CPQ started to trend up and the EMA was quicker to pick up on the recent price change and remain closer to the price.

Which is better?

Which moving average you use will depend on your trading and investing style and preferences. The simple moving average obviously has a lag, but the exponential moving average may be prone to quicker breaks. <u>Some traders prefer to use exponential moving averages for shorter time periods to capture changes quicker</u>. Some investors prefer simple moving averages over long time periods to identify long-term trend changes. In addition, much will depend on the individual security in question. A 50-day SMA might work great for identifying support levels in the NASDAQ, but a 100-day EMA may work better for the Dow Transports. Moving average type and length of time will depend greatly on the individual security and how it has reacted in the past.

The initial thought for some is that greater sensitivity and quicker signals are bound to be beneficial. This is not always true and brings up a great dilemma for the technical analyst: the trade off between sensitivity and reliability. The more sensitive an indicator is, the more signals that will be given. These signals may prove timely, but with increased sensitivity comes an increase in false signals. The less sensitive an indicator is, the fewer signals that will be given. However, less sensitivity leads to fewer and more reliable signals. Sometimes these signals can be late as well.

For moving averages, the same dilemma applies. Shorter moving averages will be more sensitive and generate more signals. The EMA, which is generally more sensitive than the SMA, will also be likely to generate more signals. However, there will also be an increase in the number of false signals and <u>whipsaws</u>. Longer moving averages will move slower and generate fewer signals. These signals will likely prove more reliable, but they also may come late. Each investor or trader should experiment with different moving average lengths and types to examine the trade-off between sensitivity and signal reliability.

Trend-Following Indicator

Moving averages smooth out a data series and make it easier to identify the direction of the trend. Because past price data is used to form moving averages, they are considered lagging, or trend following, indicators. Moving averages will not predict a change in trend, but rather follow behind the current trend. Therefore, they are best suited for trend identification and trend following purposes, not for prediction.

When to use Moving Average

Because moving averages follow the trend, they work best when a security is trending and are ineffective when a security moves in a trading range. With this in mind, investors and traders should first identify securities that display some trending characteristics before attempting to analyze with moving averages. This process does not have to be a scientific examination. Usually, a simple visual assessment of the price chart can determine if a security exhibits characteristics of trend.

In its simplest form, a security's price can be doing only one of three things: trending up, trending down or trading in a range. An uptrend is established when a security forms a series of higher highs and higher lows. A downtrend is established when a security forms a series of lower lows and lower highs. A trading range is established if a security cannot establish an uptrend or downtrend. If a security is in a trading range, an uptrend is started when the upper boundary of the range is broken and a downtrend begins when the lower boundary is broken.

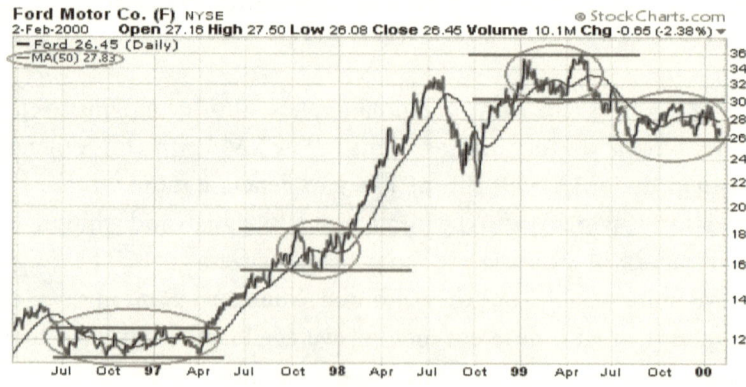

Fig. 21

In the Ford example, it is evident that a stock can go through both trending and trading phases. The red circles indicate trading range phases that are interspersed among trending periods. It is sometimes difficult to determine when a trend will stop and a trading range will begin or when a trading range will stop and a trend will begin. The basic rules for trends and trading ranges laid out above can be applied to Ford. Notice the trading range periods, the breakouts (both up and down) and the trending periods. The moving average worked well in times of trend, but faired poorly in times of trading. Also note how the moving average lags behind the trend: it is always under the price during an uptrend and above the price during a downtrend. A 50-day simple moving average was used for this example. However, the umber of periods is optional and much will depend on the characteristics of the security as the individual's trading style.

Fig. 22

If price movements are choppy and erratic over an extended period of time, then a moving average is probably not the best choice for analysis. The chart for Coca-Cola shows a security that moved from 60 to 40 in a couple months in 2001. Prior to this decline, the price gyrated above and below its moving average. After the decline, the stock continued its erratic behavior without developing much of a trend. Trying to analyze this security based on a moving average is likely to be a lesson in futility

Fig. 23

A quick look at the chart for Time Warner shows a different picture. Over the same time period, Time Warner has shown the ability to trend. There are 3 distinct trends or price movements that extend for a number of months. Once the stock moves above or below the 70-day SMA, it usually continues in that direction for a little while longer. Coca-Cola, on the other hand, broke above and below its 70-day SMA numerous times and would have been prone to numerous <u>whipsaws</u>. A longer moving average might work better, but it is clear that the Time Warner chart had better trending characteristics.

Trend Identification/Confirmation

There are three ways to identify the direction of the trend with moving averages: direction, location and crossovers.

The first trend identification technique uses the direction of the moving average to determine the trend. If the moving average is rising, the trend is considered up. If the moving average is declining, the trend is considered down. The direction of a moving average can be determined simply by looking at a plot of the moving average or by applying an indicator to the moving average. In either case, we would not want to act on every subtle change, but rather look at general directional movement and changes.

Fig. 24

In the case of Disney, a 100-day exponential moving average (EMA) has been used to determine the trend. We do not want to act on every little change in the moving average, but rather significant upturns and downturns. This is not a scientific study, but a number of significant turning points can be spotted just based on visual observation (red circles). A few good signals were rendered, but also a few whipsaws and late signals. Much of the performance would depend on your entry and exit points. The length of the moving average influences the number of signals and their timeliness. Moving averages are lagging indicators. Therefore, the longer the moving average is, the further behind the price movement it will be. For quicker signals, a 50-day EMA could have been used.

The second technique for trend identification is price location. The location of the price relative to the moving average can be used to determine the basic trend. If the price is above the moving average, the trend is considered up. If the price is below the moving average, the trend is considered down.

Fig. 25

This example is pretty straightforward. The long-term for CSCO is determined by the location of the stock relative to its 100-day SMA. When CSCO is above its 100-day SMA, the trend is considered bullish. When the stock is below the 100-day SMA, the trend is considered bearish. Buy and sell signals are generated by crosses above and below the moving average. There was a brief sell signal generated in Aug-99 and a false buy signal in July-00. Both of these signals occurred when Cisco's trend began to weaken. For the most part though, this simple method would have kept an investor in throughout most of the bull move.

The third technique for trend identification is based on the location of the shorter moving average relative to the longer moving average. If the shorter moving average is above the longer moving average, the trend is considered up. If the shorter moving average is below the longer moving average, the trend is considered to be down.

For Inter-Tel, (see chart on next page) a 30/100 moving average crossover was used to determine the trend. When the 30-day moving average moves above the 100-day moving average, the trend is considered bullish. When the 30-day moving average declines below the 100-day moving average, the trend is considered bearish. A plot of the 30/100 differential is plotted below the price chart by using the Percentage Price Oscillator (PPO) set to (30, 100, 1). When the differential is positive the trend is considered up—when it is negative the trend is considered down. As with all trend-following systems, the signals work well when the stock develops a strong trend, but are ineffective when the stock is in a trading range. Also notice that the signals tend to be late and after the move has begun. Again, trend following indicators are best for identification and following, not predicting.

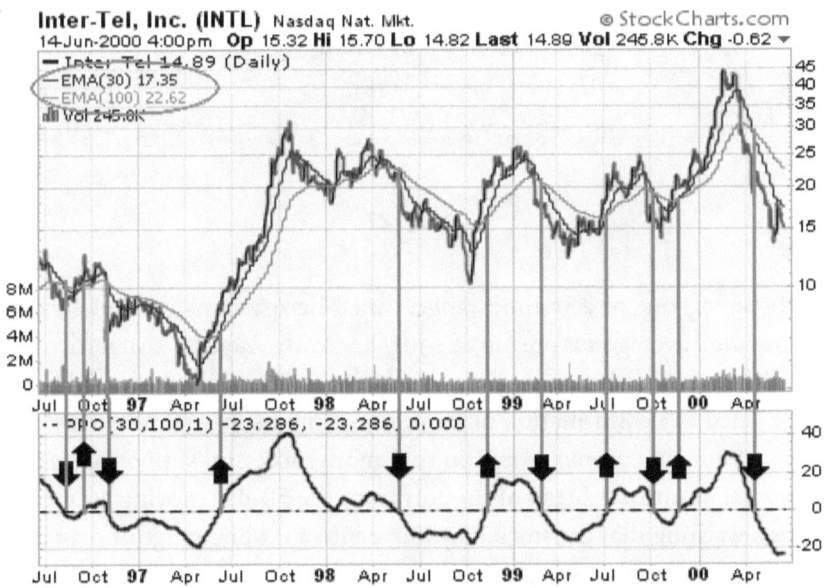

Fig. 26

Support and Resistance Levels

Another use of moving averages is to identify support and resistance levels. This is usually accomplished with one moving average and is based on historical precedent. As with trend identification, support and resistance level identification through moving averages works best in trending markets.

Fig. 27

After breaking out of a trading range, Sun Microsystems (above) successfully tested moving average support in late July and early August. Also notice that the June resistance breakout near 18 turned into support. Therefore, the moving average acted as a confirmation of <u>resistance-turned-support</u>. After this first test, the 50-day moving average went on to 4 more successful support tests over the next several months. A break of support from the 50-day moving average would serve as a warning that the stock may move into a trading range or may be about to change the direction of the trend. Such a break occurred in Apr-00 and the 50-day SMA turned into resistance later that month. When the stock broke above the 50-day SMA in early Jun-00, it returned to a support level until the Oct-00 break. In Oct-00, the 50-day SMA became a resistance level and that held for many months.

Moving Average Convergence Divergence—MACD

One modification of the traditional Moving Average is the MACD. It is specifically used to not only help define a trend but also to measure momentum. Basically, this indicator attempts to show the relationship between two moving averages of prices. The MACD is calculated by subtracting the 26-day exponential moving average (EMA) from the 12-day EMA. A nine-day EMA of the MACD, called the "signal line", is then plotted on top of the MACD, functioning as a trigger for buy and sell signals.

There are three common methods used to interpret the MACD[7]:

1. Crossovers—As shown in the chart below, <u>when the MACD *falls* below the signal line, it is a bearish signal</u>, which indicates that it may be time to sell. Conversely, <u>when the MACD *rises* above the signal line, the indicator gives a bullish signal, which suggests that the price of the asset is likely to experience upward momentum</u>. Many traders wait for a confirmed cross above the signal line before entering into a position to avoid getting getting "faked out" or entering into a position too early, as shown by the first arrow.

2. Divergence—When the security price diverges from the MACD. It signals the end of the current trend.

3. Dramatic rise—When the MACD rises dramatically—that is, the shorter moving average pulls away from the longer-term moving average—it is a signal that the security is overbought and will soon return to normal levels.

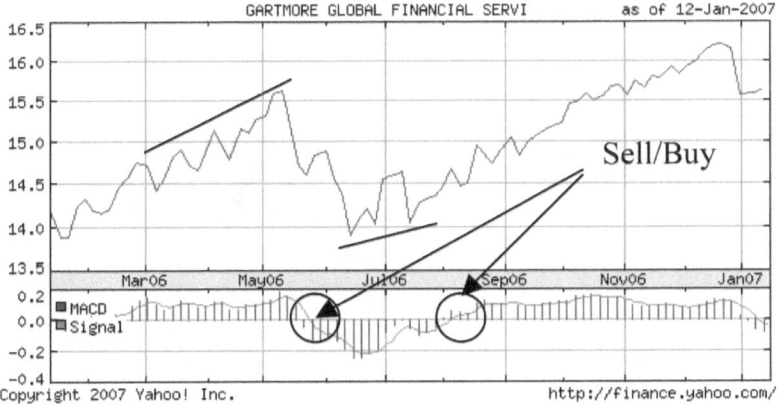

Fig. 28

7   Investopedia.com

On Balance Volume

Developed by the once favored stock market guru, Joseph Granville, On Balance Volume is a very useful tool to help gauge sentiment about a particular stock or option by presenting a picture of what is happening between price movement and demand. If volume supports price increase, it shows a demand driven movement. However, if the price is moving up but volume is declining, this shows a divergence and may indicate a reversal.

On the flip side, if price is declining and volume is also decreasing, this may also signal a reversal to the upside. In few words, a trend needs to be fueled by volume. When the fuel runs low, the ability to sustain the trend is diminished. Use of the On Balance Volume is an excellent confirmation tool to use with other indicators.

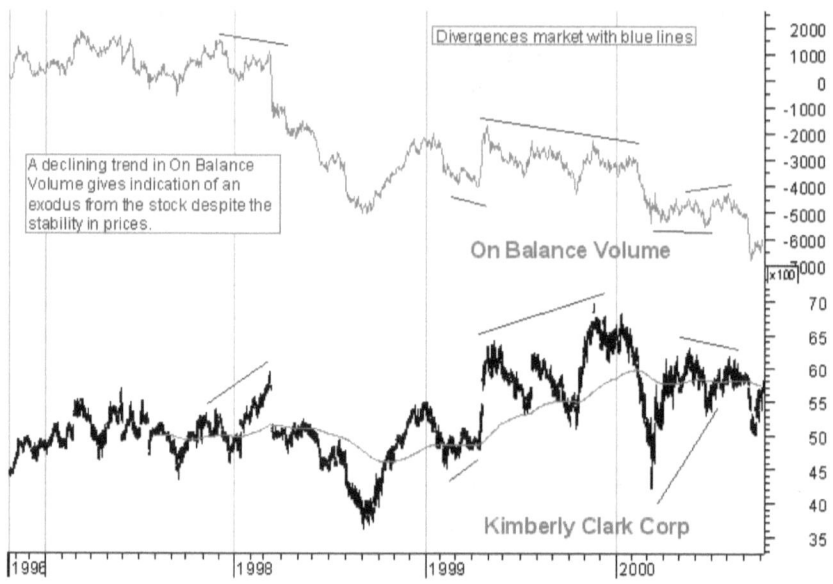

Fig. 29

Bollinger Bands

Bollinger Bands are the brain child of John Bollinger, a noted technical analyst. Bollinger Bands consist of a centerline and two price channels (Fig. 30), one above the centerline and one below. The centerline is an <u>exponential moving average</u>, and the price channels are standard deviations of the stock the chartist is studying. The bands will expand and contract as the price action of an issue becomes volatile (expansion) or becomes bound into a tight trading pattern (contraction). Thus, at a glance, the Bollinger Bands can demonstrate the amount of volatility of the price movement. When the bands contract around the moving average, trading is less volatile. When the bands expand, volatility is increasing. One could say that when the Bollinger Bands start to bulge, that means some sort of pressure is building up and some movement may push through the band indicating a significant movement. As long as prices do not move out of Bollinger Band channel, the trader can be reasonably confident that prices are moving as expected. <u>But when prices start to hug close to the band, it can mean an *overbought* (upper band) or *oversold* (lower band) condition.</u> In other words, a <u>trend reversal is possible</u>.

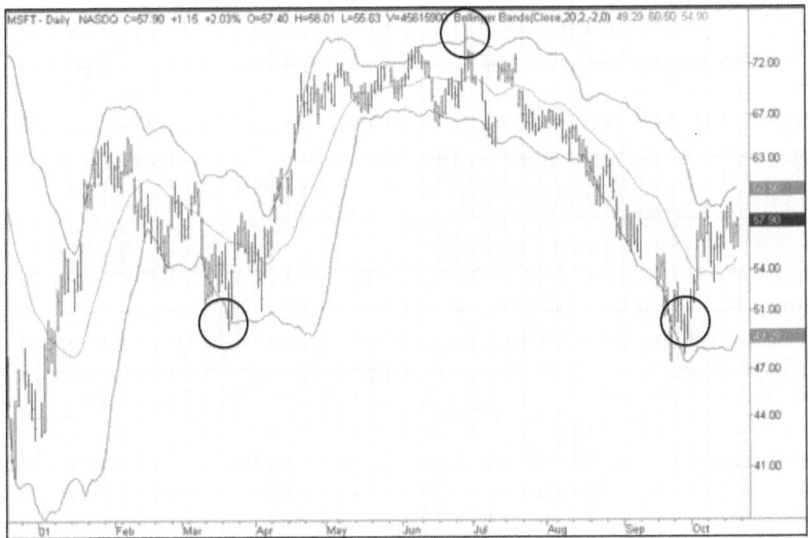

Fig. 30

As in all indicators, other indicators should provide confirmation. In the case of Bollinger Bands, the On Balance Volume indicator can provide good verification.

Relative Strength Index[8]

The Relative Strength Index (RSI), an oscillator developed by Welles Wilder, measures the momentum strength of a stock by monitoring changes in its closing prices. The formula for RSI is as follows:

$$RSI = 100-[100/(1 + RS)]$$

Where: RS = average of upward price change over a select number of days/ average of downward price change over the same number of days

RSI fluctuates between 0 and 100. RSI peaks indicate overbought levels and suggest price tops, while RSI troughs denote oversold levels and share price bottoms.

Two horizontal reference lines are normally placed at 30 (indicating an oversold area) and 70 (indicating an overbought area). These reference lines can be adjusted depending on the market environment. Some analysts move these lines to 40 and 80 in bull markets (raising the bar, so to speak) and lower them to 20 and 60 in bear markets.

It is advised that traders use the "five-percent" rule—RSI spends less than five percent of the time beyond either reference line over a six-month period. You can adjust these reference lines every three months (once per quarter).

There is no "holy grail" level dictating guaranteed overbought or oversold readings. RSI can stay overbought in bull markets and oversold in bear markets for prolonged periods. Like most indicators, you will become accustomed to using RSI, getting a "feel" for what works best for you.

Divergence

The most significant signal is generated on "bullish" or "bearish" divergences between the RSI and the price of the underlying stock. A bullish divergence

---

8   Schaeffer Research

gives a "buy" or long signal and occurs <u>when the stock price makes a new near-term low, but the RSI makes a shallower trough relative to the previous decline</u> (see Fig. 31). <u>You would enter a long position as soon as the RSI turns upward from this second bottom.</u>

The buy signal is especially strong if the first RSI low drops below the oversold reference line. This indicates that selling pressure is near exhaustion and a directional change (upward) is imminent.

Note in the chart (Fig. 31) that blue arrows indicate long or buy signals. The circled trough in the RSI reading indicates the "previous decline" that did move below the lower reference line.

A higher trough in the RSI accompanied the subsequent low in the stock. The upside move was explosive. A bearish divergence that gives a "sell" or short signal occurs when prices rally to a new near-term peak but the RSI makes a lower peak than during the previous advance by the stock. This calls for selling short or purchasing a put option as soon as the RSI turns down from this second peak. Place a protective stop above the stock's latest minor high. Sell signals are especially strong if the first RSI peak is above the upper or overbought reference line.

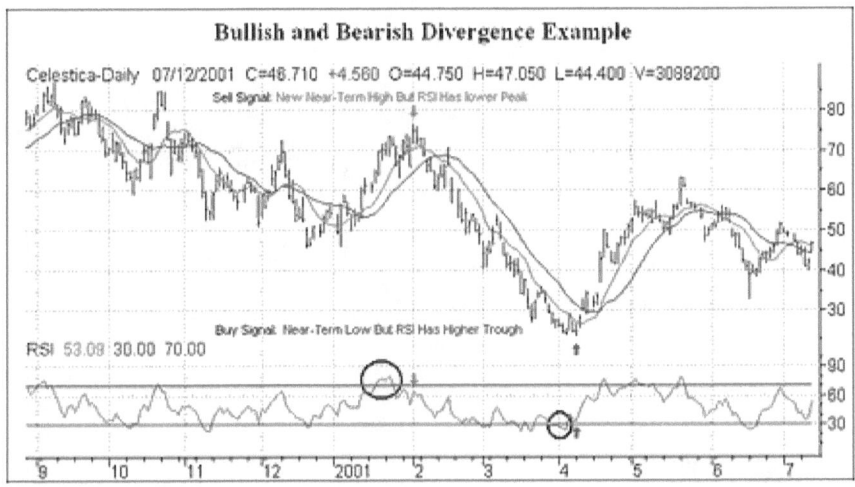

Fig. 31

Note in the chart above that the red arrows indicate short or sell signals. The circled RSI peak coincides with the previous advance that moved above the upper reference line. A lower peak in the RSI accompanied the subsequent higher peak in the stock. Note how the substantial downside move was predicted by the RSI.

Charting Patterns

Classical charting methods work well if filtered with the RSI. The RSI indicator can be used to validate trend lines, support/resistance, and even reversal patterns. Since the RSI is a leading or coincident indicator (never a lagging indicator), <u>it can be used to anticipate the completions of these patterns.</u>

The Ann Taylor Stores (ANN) chart below (Fig. 32) illustrates how RSI can validate a pattern or trend line. In this example, we are judging whether Ann's short-term 10-day (red line) and 20-day (blue line) moving averages will offer expected support or resistance. Note in the lower half of the chart the RSI's trend of higher highs and higher lows that was supported by the up trending red trend line. During this period, the shares tested and moved up off their 10-day moving average. The RSI then started to roll over, as evidenced by a series of lower peaks and lower troughs with the peaks capped by the declining black trend line. During this period, the stock proceeded to waffle around its daily moving averages. After failing these trend lines, a subsequent test rejected the shares lower.

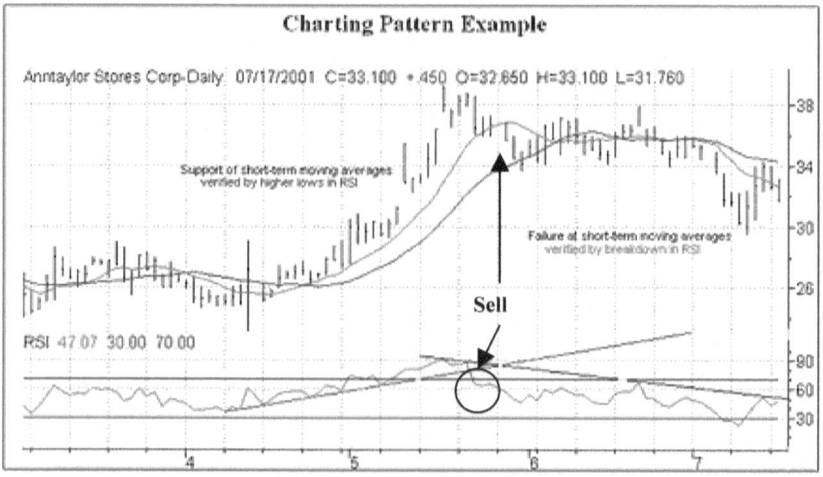

Fig. 32

Reversals

Buy/sell signals can also be obtained simply by following the RSI levels. These signals should be verified by the prevalent trend in the stock. As the RSI rises above the upper reference line, bulls are in control but the stock is considered overbought and is likely vulnerable to selling pressure. <u>When the RSI falls back below the reference line, a sell signal is generated.</u>

If the RSI moves below the lower reference line, the bears are in charge, but the stock is considered to be likely oversold and entering a "buy" zone. When the RSI reverses back above the lower reference line, a buy signal is generated. (One word of caution—<u>doesn't "fade" or bet against the prevailing trend of the stock or market</u>.)

<u>Caution: Stocks in strong up trends tend to stay overbought, while stocks in strong downtrends tend to hold their oversold RSI readings.</u> Buying when the RSI turns up from an oversold area (blue circles) and selling when the RSI reverses from an overbought condition (red circles) can allow a trader to profit from quick moves in either direction. Be cautioned, however, that this is <u>the least effective use of this indicator</u>.

Put-Call Ratio

Akin to RSI, but a little bit different is The Put-Call Ratio. Like the RSI, it is an indicator which measure how investors and speculators feel about the direction of price movement. If there are more Puts than Calls, investors feel that the direction is down (bearish). On the contrary, if there are more Calls than Puts, the feeling is that prices will go up (bullish).

The ratio is calculated by dividing the number of traded <u>put options</u> by the number of traded <u>call options</u>. A moving average tracking the P-C ratio for equities or Indices can be used to watch for strength or changes in sentiment. When the ratio of put-to-call volume gets too high (meaning more puts traded relative to calls) the market is ready for a reversal to the upside and has typically been in a bearish decline. And when the ratio gets too low (meaning more calls traded relative to puts), the market is ready for a reversal to the downside (as was the case in early 2000). That is to say, the P-C ratio can be used as a contrarian indicator. If the ratio is getting too high, that means that the market may be getting oversold and will soon go up. Likewise, if the P-C ratio is steadily getting smaller (P/C getting smaller means C is getting larger), the market may be getting overbought and may soon come down.

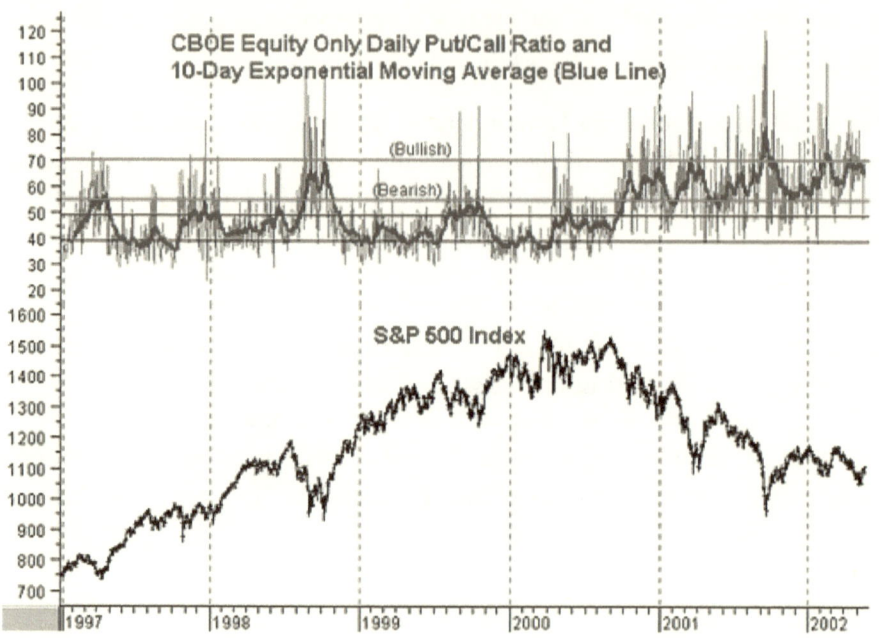

Fig. 33
Created using Metastock Professional. Data Source: Pinnacle IDX

Remember, the higher the ratio, the higher the amount of puts purchased vs. calls. (more investors feel that the prices will be in a downward direction.). As we saw with the RSI, an over sold condition is when the EMA for the P/C ratio goes above the upper band and a buy call signal is generated when the EMA moves back across the upper band in a downward direction. The reverse would be true when the EMA goes below the lower band; revealing an over bought condition and when the MA crosses the lower band in an upward direction a buy put signal would be generated. (P/C therefore as C gets larger, the ratio gets smaller). But one of the main reasons that we cover a multiple of indicators is that we want several indicators to provide verification.

An important observation is that portfolio managers routinely purchase index options to help hedge and as a result will distort the "sentiment" factor of using a put-call ratio. Therefore, <u>it is best to use the p/c ratio for equities only</u>.

Open Interest

Open Interest is a term that all option traders should understand. When a trader buys a call or put it requires the opening of a contract. This creates an "open interest". When the call or put is sold to "close out" the opening contract the open interest created by the purchase no longer exists. The same holds true when writing (selling) a put or call. The important fact is that there must be an offsetting transaction to close out the open interest.

What is the significance of open interest?

If there is above average open interest, that usually means there is a stronger than normal interest in the option—regardless of what direction the price is moving. <u>Thus, higher open interest adds support to the trend</u>. However, if there is high open interest and not much movement of the option it could signal an over bought situation (put or call). Also, another concern is what would happen if all those open interest contracts all start to stampede to get closed out? Would there be enough interest on the other side of the close-out transaction?

So, open interest can be used to verify and support a trend if there is a correlation with the increasing open interest and increasing trend (either up or down) <u>but open interest can also be a danger signal if the price and open interest movement correlation is not there</u>.

What is the connection between open interest and volume?

<u>Volume is the number of contracts traded. Open Interest is the number of contracts still open and working, i.e., not closed out.</u> To give you a very simplistic example, let's say today is the first trading day for an option. So, today, 1 contract is bought. Thus, volume is 1 and open interest is 1. Tomorrow, another 1 contract is bought, thus volume is 1, but open interest is now 2. The day after that, both contracts are sold and closed out, thus volume is 2, open interest is 0.

An important distinction between the two is that volume is a good indicator of liquidity of the option but open interest does not. As a matter of fact, <u>if there is high open interest and low volume it could signal a potential problem getting out of the position.</u>

Stock screening software programs

In the "good old days" before computers, technical analysis was a painstaking and time consuming process but today there is a plethora of excellent and inexpensive stock screening programs which will subject a stock to an exhaustive numerical analysis and do everything except make the final decision. Advisory services will offer to do it all (except pay for the premium, of course). A great company for premium Stock and Stock Option picks are ThinkNTrade.com.

Summary of Chapter 2

- Fundamental analysis is focused on the financial fundamentals of the company and the "story" of the business and its potential within its sector.

- Technical analysis is concerned with the interpretation of charts and mathematical analysis of historical data based upon the underlying asset and the option itself.

- A Technical Analyst tries to develop objective information on which to base a mechanical system to evaluate an opportunity.

- There are numerous tools used in technical analysis but some of the most common are: channel analysis, simple moving averages, exponential moving averages, MACD, On Balance Volume, Bollinger Bands, Put-Call ratios, Volume and Open Interest.

- There are many good stock screening programs which can quickly sort out potential candidates but it is how the information is interpreted and verified that makes the difference. Experienced traders learn what works for them and develop a disciplined approach to each trade but almost all technical analysis use some or all of the methods introduced in Chapter 2.

CHAPTER 3

Developing a System and Choosing
an Option to Trade

We've covered many of the important tools to help analyze a potential trade. But before getting started in putting together a methodology, we should discuss the fundamental elements of establishing a trading system.

Many traders prefer to shop around for a "turnkey" system to purchase or others prefer to develop their own system. Whichever you choose, you must consider several things first:

Define your objectives

- Can you trade full-time or only part-time?

    If you are new to trading, it's probably a good idea to start part-time so you can develop your trading skills and a system. You'll need to devote at least a couple of hours each day until you become proficient and comfortable with the trading milieu. After gaining enough experience, you can decide whether or not you want to become a full-time trader.

- Are you looking for cash flow or capital appreciation?

    If you are trying to make a living as a trader, cash flow to live on is your main objective. If that is the case, you'll need to devote your full time to trading activities. A day trader tries to make many successful trades with small profit margins. This strategy requires full attention and a concern for capital preservation. If you are more interested in capital growth, you'll be looking for higher profit margins and less trading activity. In either case, research and tracking require your full attention.

- How much money can you devote to trading?

  Establish how much of your trading capital you can afford to lose without affecting your ability to live your current lifestyle. If you are trading with money that you may need, that can greatly affect your trading psychology in that the pressure can be intense and it is hard to maintain the discipline and psychological "cool" that a trading system requires.

  You'll find that as you gain confidence in your system and your skills, your risk tolerance will increase. But when you are new to trading, you need to have the time to develop your comfort level and make sure you don't run out of money before you get your trading "sea legs".

- What return are you looking for?

  If you are a day trader, how much cash flow do you need to generate to meet your living expenses? For example: If you require $4,000 net per month, you'll need to generate at least $5,600 in trading profits per month because you must take into account taxes and commissions. Divide this number by the number of trading days per month (20) and you will need to generate at least $280 per trading day.

  If you are a part-time trader, you may be looking for a certain percent profit on each trade. Keep in mind that small profits each month can add up to an impressive total percent return for a year. For instance, if you can manage just a 6% monthly net profit on your trades it would translate into over 70% annual return. Trading is not about hitting home runs but hitting for average.

Once you decide on your level of commitment, you then have a better idea of what system might be best for you. But regardless of what manner of trading strategy you plan to use, it must be applied in a systematic and disciplined manner.

The central idea behind having a disciplined system is to avoid the perils of emotion affecting how and when you trade. Fear of failure must be overcome before it becomes fear of losing money. Once you see that your system can bring positive results a majority of the time, your fear of losing money will not be a distraction and destroy confidence in your system. In other words, a systematic and disciplined implementation of your system will help null the negative influence of your fears or exuberance. All of this sounds logical and rather obvious but if you don't use the restraint that a system that is matched properly with your goals can provide, you will probably not be happy with the results of your trading.

Every system begins with selection. First, are you looking for short term and small profits or are you looking for larger return over a longer period. The time period is critical because this establishes the range of the charts and data that you will be looking at. For instance, if you are looking for small profits in a short period, you may be looking at charts that track data by the minute (most day traders are minute by minute). For the purpose of this book, we will assume that you are a part-time trader and you are looking for trades which may take as long as two to three months to develop. Let's say your profit goal is 20% net commissions. Let's follow an imaginary trade.

Sample of a long call trade

The following is a step by step example of how a typical analysis of a potential candidate for an option trade could be done. There are numerous trading systems and this methodology is only one way but whatever system you choose should be applied in a disciplined manner on every trade.

1. The first thing you need to know is: what is happening with the market in general. Is it in an uptrend, flat or trending down? "Never fight the trend" is a cliché for a very good reason.

2. Now you look for a stock that has two obvious requirements: 1) a stock that has an option derivative; 2) a stock that is in an obvious trend, which is in synch with the direction of the market (up trend—in the case of a call). Also, we would want to know what the Beta of the stock is. Traders prefer higher Betas. Many traders use one of the many good screening programs, advisory services, or other sources to help doing a search and screening of the many thousands of possible candidates.

3. Once a potential stock is located—in this example we use Microsoft (MSFT), we look at longer period charts to see the long term trend. Is the trend just beginning or has it been trending for a long time? In the case of Microsoft, it has been in an uptrend for some time—as had the market in general.

4.   Reduce the chart time periods to look for shorter term trends within the long term trend.

Fig. 35

In the above chart, there seems to be a shorter term cycle that appears to last approximately three weeks. We see that the current up move is nearing the middle of a short term cycle.

5.   Now we run a <u>Bollinger Band test</u> to check for a potential overbought situation.

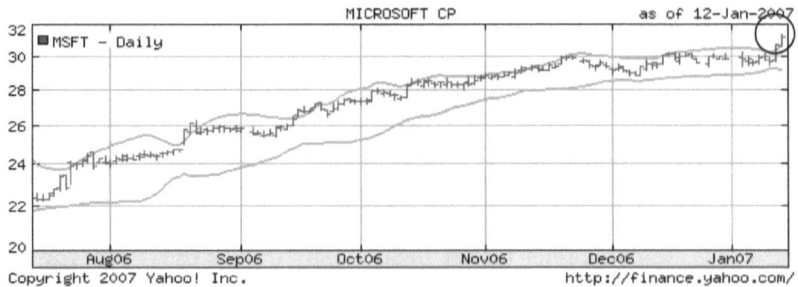

Fig. 36

We see that the price has broken out of the upper Bollinger Band and signals a possible overbought situation. Our enthusiasm for the breakout is now tempered. We will look for verification from some other tools.

6. <u>Now we check for MACD</u>. As we recall, MACD tells us about trend and momentum. We are looking for a movement above the signal line if we are going to be long call or a movement below the signal line if we are going long put.(we do not fight the up trend so we are not looking for a put).

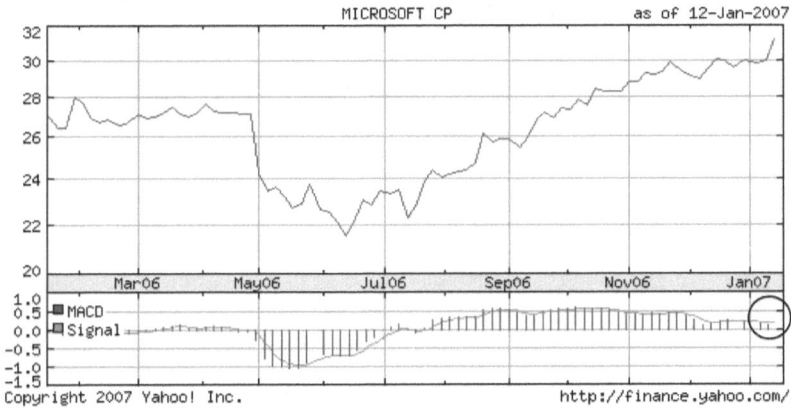

Fig.37

In the example above, the MACD is far below the signal line.

7. We look into our tool box and pull out an <u>RSI (Relative Strength Indicator)</u>.

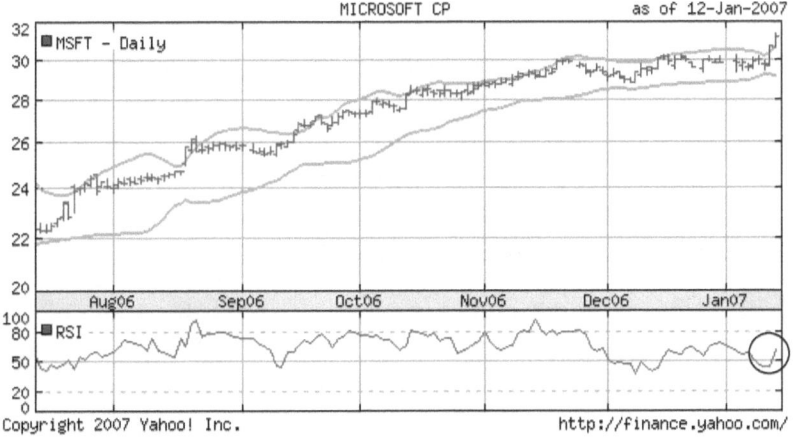

Fig. 38

We see that the RSI has taken a sharp turn toward the overbought line but has not reached a critical level yet (above 80%).

8. We decide we need to look for another form of verification so we take a look at volume. The spike up in volume also speaks of possible overbuying (lower panel).

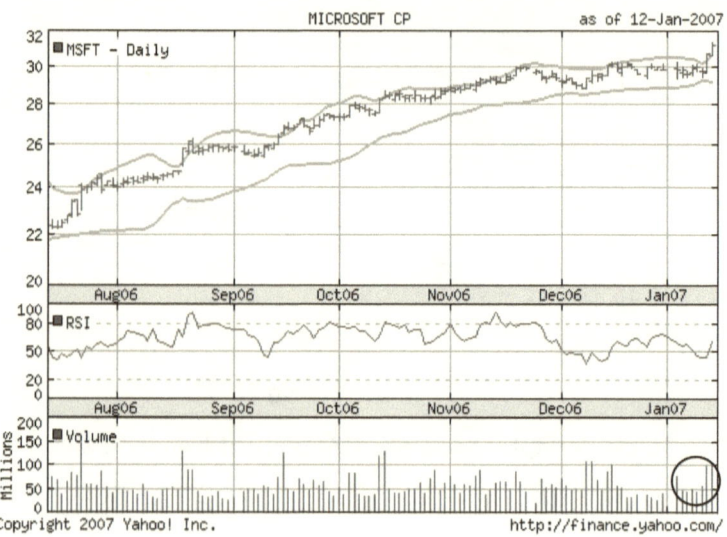

Fig. 39

We see that volume has spiked supporting the upside break-out but also supporting the Bollinger Band oversold signal. RSI is far above a buy signal. At this point, we see risk of an overbought situation but at the same time we want to know if something fundamental has happened to propel the stock upward for a sustained up move. We turn to some fundamental information on MSFT.

9. Now we check some fundamentals about the stock. We find that a very positive article was written about MSFT in a newspaper of a large city. The particular editorial views Microsoft as the dominant player in a developing technology. This one article seems to be the reason for the breakout! One person, who may even own the stock, writes an editorial about the potential future of the company. Other

than this article, we can't find another fundamental reason why the stock has spiked.

10. At this point, we have seen enough to make a decision. <u>MSFT is not a good candidate for a long call.</u>

11. Why not?
    1. The price has broken through the <u>upper Bollinger Band</u>. This is a sign of a possible overbought situation.
    2. MACD is far below a buy signal
    3. The RSI has also made a sharp upturn toward an overbought situation.
    4. Volume also shows signs of an overbought status as it has spiked to an abnormal amount as compared to recent history.
    5. The price seems to be peaking at the middle of a short cycle and will probably make a short term correction.

12. What would have made MSFT a good candidate for a long call?
    1. Price moving through the <u>lower Bollinger Band</u>
    2. MACD crossing the signal line in an upward direction.
    3. RSI at or below the 20% line
    4. A moderate increase in volume
    5. Short term cycle nearing its end.

Keep in mind, the process explained in the example above is just an example of one systematic way to analyze a potential candidate. Each system may have its own methodology but the important thing is to find a system that has a track record that works—*most of the time.*

Let's suppose that MSFT had the indications of being a good candidate, what would be the next steps?

1. Look at the <u>option chain</u> for a good call option to buy.(see Fig. 40 below)

CALL OPTIONS   **Strike Price at 30.00**

Expires	Symbol	Last	Chg	Bid	Ask	Vol	Open Int
Jan 07	MSQAK.X	**1.23**	⬆0.39	1.20	1.25	17,285	255,512
Feb 07	MSQBK.X	**1.70**	⬆0.35	1.65	1.70	9,817	18,002
Apr 07	MSQDK.X	**2.20**	⬆0.40	2.15	2.20	1,908	123,737
Jul 07	MSQGK.X	**2.80**	⬆0.30	2.80	2.85	1,264	21,376
Jan 08	WMFAF.X	**3.77**	⬆0.37	3.70	3.80	434	361,769
Jan 09	VMFAF.X	**5.30**	⬆0.40	5.20	5.30	7,330	60,545

PUT OPTIONS   **Strike Price at 30.00**

Expires	Symbol	Last	Chg	Bid	Ask	Vol	Open Int
Jan 07	MSQMK.X	**0.05**	⬇0.10	N/A	0.05	7,202	83,251
Feb 07	MSQNK.X	**0.44**	⬇0.09	0.40	0.45	1,723	10,215
Apr 07	MSQPK.X	**0.65**	⬇0.18	0.65	0.70	322	41,166
Jul 07	MSQSK.X	**1.05**	⬇0.25	1.05	1.10	73	9,801
Jan 08	WMFMF.X	**1.50**	⬇0.20	1.50	1.55	228	66,136
Jan 09	VMFMF.X	**2.30**	⬇0.45	2.15	2.25	3	27,727

Highlighted options are in-the-money.

Fig. 40.   Option Chain for MSFT: Current price: $31.21

2. In-the-money calls are usually more expensive so we might want to look
    for something just a little out-of-the money but with enough liquidity
    (volume). Some traders feel that it is better to buy in-the-money calls

to take advantage of momentum and get in and get out quickly once the profit target has been hit. Others seem to prefer to buy out-of-the-money contracts because they are less expensive and help to conserve capital. Experience and the amount of money you have to invest will determine whether you will be an "in-the-money" or "out-of-the-money" trader.

3. Once you find a contract month with the strike price and premium you feel most comfortable with, you make sure to check the open interest and volume of contracts history. Will there be enough liquidity if you want to close out your position? Don't buy a contract that lacks at least moderate volume. In the chain below, we see in-the-money (calls) are pretty inexpensive. (Note the increasing time value premium for the further out months.) The fact that the in-the-money calls are inexpensive shows that the market seems not to feel too strongly about the possibilities of the option being a real winner in that there doesn't seem to be much demand or the price would probably be much higher for an ITM option.

In this example of MSFT, we would not buy a call. Also, we would not buy a put (unless we wanted to hedge a long position) because the trend of the market and the stock is up. Never fight the trend.

As we mentioned, there are a ton of systems and programs on the market, which will use specific parameters and tools to screen for opportunities. If you do buy a program or subscribe to an advisory service, you should understand what philosophy and parameters are being used in the screening and decision making process. Using a canned system is an excellent way to start trading but you should understand how it works and what kind of track record the system has produced. We will discuss "getting started" later in the book.

Summary of Chapter 3

- Technical analysis looks at the statistical history of price and other associated data to provide a series of indicators, which help to make an objective decision about an underlying security. If the analysis shows an opportunity, we then decide whether or not to purchase an in-the-money or slightly out-of-the-money option.

- When we decide to implement a system, we use it in a disciplined manner and try to "filter out" any "hype". However, we do take a look at some fundamentals of the stock to see if there are any political-economic events that might have an immediate affect.

- If there is any doubt, move on. There are thousands of stocks to pick from.

- Have a profit goal and close-out the position when it is reached. Don't be greedy.

- Make sure that the option you choose has enough trading to guarantee some liquidity.

- If the position you take doesn't act like you think it should, cut your losses quickly.

- The example trade we used had a system which required that certain things happen for a call position to be taken:

  1. Trend of underlying stock and general market in the same direction
  2. Bollinger Bands prices are along the lower band.
  3. MACD crosses the signal line in an upward direction (long call)
  4. RSI is near the bottom range
  5. Volume supporting price movement. (but not overbought)

We could have used other methods and indicators but this is an example of only one way. A system should always be implemented in a disciplined manner and no deviations taken unless you are intentionally modifying your system.

We mentioned that a good way to start out trading is to look for a system or advisory service with a proven track record and one you can fully understand. Go to ThinkNTrade.com.

CHAPTER 4

Money Management

"Money management is the process of analyzing trades for risk and potential profits, determining how much risk, if any, is acceptable and managing a trade position (if taken) to control risk and maximize profitability." Investopedia

What is Drawdown?

If you start investing with $5,000 and you lose $1,000 your "Drawdown" is 20% of your investing funds. If you then made back that $1,000 your Drawdown would be back to zero. Pretty simple, but making up for Drawdown is a little more complicated.

From our example above, we lost $1,000 which leaves a balance of $4,000 in our investing account. To get back to zero Drawdown, we have to make a profit of 25% ($4000 x 1.25 = $5000.) So, our original 20% loss requires a 25% gain to get back to our original $5,000 investment (zero Drawdown). But what is worse is that as losses increase the percentage gain to offset those losses grows geometrically. For instance, a 50% loss in equity requires a 100% profit to recover the Drawdown! Refer to Fig. 41.

% Drawdown	% gain required to recoup losses
10	11.11
20	25.00
30	42.85
40	66.66
50	100
60	150
70	233
80	400
90	900
100	Busted

Fig. 41

The obvious message of this rather disturbing table is: <u>avoid losing money</u>.

After becoming familiar with the math of drawdown recovery, it should become obvious that the risk of losing money will have a major impact on trading strategy. Too much effort may be given to finding the system that will pick the winners instead of maybe staying away from the losers. In fact, this is why money management is so important. It's not only about winning but also very much about not losing what you have gained.

How to avoid losing money

You can't. Plane and simple … if you trade you will lose. The key is to limit losses. Don't expect to win much over 50% of the trades you make. But the main focus is to limit the size of losses and cut losses aggressively. It is not unreasonable to win less than 50% of your trades but to make an excellent annual return on your portfolio.

Most of us are taught in our society that 95% is good and 70% at the edge of bad. As a trader you must get over that view and understand that keeping your losses to a minimum and compounding gains is the real name of the trading game. In other words, if you can maintain you're losses at an average of 5%–9% and an average of 15%–20% on your gains, and you have a 50% win ratio, you would be a very happy camper. It become a matter of how one limits risks and conserves gains that is the key to being successful over the long run. We turn our attention to the specifics of how we can "stay in the game".

Allocation

Courtney Smith writes in his book, <u>New Thinking in Technical Analysis: Trading Models from the Masters</u>, a system of "Fixed Fractional Bet" is discussed wherein any trade will represent a fixed percent of the total investment funds available.

For example, let's say you have $25,000 available for options trading and you wish to allocate 10 percent of your total account to <u>each trade</u>. You would therefore trade $2,500 for your first trade. Assume the trade gains 80 percent, or a $2,000 profit. Because your account size is now $27,000, your next trade would be for $2,700 (0.1*27,000). Now let's say your first trade lost 40 percent (remember you need to let your winners run and cut your more numerous losses short), or $1,000. Your account would now stand at $24,000, meaning that you would allocate only $2,400 to your next trade. Notice how this differs from a fixed-dollar strategy in which you would invest $2,500 in each trade.

This is just an example of a system to help maintain discipline and help limit exposure to losses. Again, the goal is to have enough money to make enough trades to compound gains and limit losses over the long term (12 months for traders). In the Fixed Fractional bet system we have more money in the market when moving up and less money exposed when things are moving down. Don't vary the percentages; don't double up when things are going your way. Pick a course and stay on it.

Limiting losses on trades

Keeping in mind that you'll probably lose more trades than win, you want to be quick to pull the plug on a trade that doesn't develop like we want it to. Set a target "punch-out price" and if your trade hits that target it is an automatic close out. Don't let your ego convince you that you should give it a chance to act like you want it to. Get out now!

For Example: You have $8,000 in your trading account. You have decided that your Fixed Fractional percentage for trading is 12%. You analysis leads to a trade in Home Depot Calls currently priced at $3.50. At your limit of 12% you can purchase $960 worth of contracts. Rounding off, you purchase 3 contracts ($1050). You set a mental stop loss of 6%, which would mean that if the contract price goes down 21 cents ($3.50x.06) or below $3.21 you would close out the position. Your maximum loss would be $63 for the three contracts. In the real world, you must also include the costs of commissions in your calculations. (You can see why it's important to shop around for the best commission prices but with good execution). Commissions are an important cost because you will be making many trades.

As you see from the example, a fairly slight downward movement and you are out of the trade. You can also see that trading options requires constant vigilance. Moreover, there will be many times when you won't close out at precisely your target stop loss due to the fact that the actual price you sell your contracts for may be lower than the target. Thus, getting good execution from your broker is almost as important as the cost of commissions.

Other considerations

- As a general rule profit targets should be at least 2 or 3 times the risk target. For example, if you are using a risk factor of 6% you should use a profit target of at least 18%.
- If you experience a "windfall" situation, consider taking some profits on the way up.
- If you make a lot of trades, consider reducing your risk target per trade.
- Don't place your "punch-out price" (stop-loss) too tight on a trade with high volatility.
- Never add to a losing position in hopes to recoup your losses.
- Don't let your drawdown exceed 30% of your trading account. If it does, take up tennis.
- After a string of losses, stop and re-evaluate your system.
- If you get too nervous or are losing sleep over your trades, stop trading.

Maybe we put the cart before the horse, but let's do some pretty basic "due diligence" when it comes to becoming a new trader or investor. The question: Are you in a financial position to trade or invest? Ask yourself the following questions.

- ❖ *Do you have a budget?* Make a realistic budget and track your expenses. Most people do this "intuitively", but actual tracking is much more effective.
- ❖ *Do you have at least 3–6 months living expenses immediately available?* This amount is most preferably in the form of cash but if you have something you can sell quickly and turn into cash, that can count.
- ❖ *Do you have a retirement plan at work?* If you do, do you contribute regularly to it. This is one of the best ways to invest because most

plans are tax deferred (you pay no taxes until you reach a certain age and start withdrawals). Also, many plans provide that employers will match a certain percentage of what the employee contributes up to a certain amount. There are plans where an employer will match 25% of what the employee contributes up to a certain amount. That means that the employee is assured of at least a 25% return on contributions! What a deal!

❖ *Do you have adequate insurance incase you become ill or incapacitated?* If you are a family man, do you have adequate life insurance?

❖ Are you ready to not touch your investment portfolio except in an emergency? Let the <u>power of compounding your gains</u> work for you. If you are going to be a day trader and hopefully make enough from trading to meet your daily expenses, will you be able to hold to your daily budget and not rob the cookie jar?

Money management is all about minimizing risk by quickly cutting losses and having at least a "win multiple" of at least 2.0. This means your average gains net at least twice as much as your losses. Example: If your average loss is 6% you should at least have an average gain of 12%. The next critical factor is your win frequency. This is where stock analysis and a good system come in. But no matter what system you use, you will have losses. It's just a matter of probability. If you find you are losing more than you have anticipated you can reduce your number of trades and acceptable loss percent. Some traders use as low as 2% loss as their stop loss. So, you can see how you manage your money is almost as important as being a high percentage winner.

Key elements of becoming a successful trader are that you need to develop a disciplined and consistent method of stock analysis and also have a disciplined and consistent money management methodology. Backing up your methods is your "trading ego," which we will discuss in the next chapter.

Summary of Chapter 4

In this chapter we learned about the importance of money management and how critical it is to limit losses and design a strategy which will allow the trader to "stay in the game.

- Recouping losses requires a geometric effort. Example: If you suffer a 50% draw-down of your investment capital, it will require a 100% profit on the balance to get back to zero drawdown.
- Even with a good system for picking winning positions, the vagaries of variation and probability will still claim you as a victim. You will lose trades.
- The key is to reduce losses to a minimum by having a close stop loss target and take action without letting emotions getting in the way. When you have a profitable trade, the profit margin should be at least 2 to 3 times the loss percentage.
- Before each trade, you should have a predetermined stop-loss and a profit target.
- Take partial profits when passing thorough profit target.
- You can be a winner even if you lose the majority of your trades if losses are minimal as compared to winning trades.
- It is vital that you risk a small portion of your trading capital on any trade. Some traders use as little as 2% of the account for trading. As a general rule of thumb, 6–12% of your capital should be used at any one time.
- If you sustain more than a 30% drawdown, you should probably stop trading and review your system and methodology.
- Stick to your system.
- Before trading, do a self-assessment of your financial position. Go to ThinkNTrade.com to help you.

CHAPTER 5

Trading Psychology

How do we know when our feelings convey real information for trading and when they merely provide interference from our conflicts over success/failure, risk/safety, etc.? Developing trading expertise is not so simple as following such slogans as "tune out your emotions when you are trading".

Many of our perceptions are colored by experience. Maybe we grew up in a family where money was a scarce resource and we learned to revere that rare but necessary commodity. Maybe we grew up in a family where money was no problem and the mystique and fear of it was not a factor. Perhaps we learned that money is only a means of keeping score and nothing more. All of us are a little different and those of us who worship money are deathly afraid of it; we put it on a pedestal and the thought of losing any is unthinkable. Or maybe we don't deem ourselves worthy of having the good things in life and thus believe that we really have no chance to better ourselves.

There is an endless amount of psychobabble to hint at what we may really think about money but to the trader, it is merely data ;cold, life-less and it's only meaning is in keeping score. If you worship money, trading may make you writhe with anxiety. But what is "money" anyway? To a millionaire, $10,000 is not that impressive. To a day laborer, it is a fortune. That is why it is important to marginalize the pain of losing money by making the amount we trade a rather insignificant part of our financial world.

We should trade money that is not necessary for our well being; and of that small and insignificant amount, we will only trade a fraction. Once you decide on what amount is appropriate for you, imagine how you would feel if you lost all of it. If you feel not the least bit uncomfortable, the money issue is no longer.

The basic idea that all a trader has to do is find a system; test it; if it gets the results you are looking for, just stick with the system in a disciplined manner. Easy! But if it were indeed that easy, everybody would be a trader.

It's a well known fact that most traders set up rules only to violate them until their demise. As psychologist Ruth Barrons Roosevelt states: "Traders and investors hang onto losing positions until the enormity of the loss overwhelms them. They sell their winning positions quickly to pocket slender profits, while the trades go on to make enormous profits. They write trading rules, only to violate them. They get greedy and over-trade, only to lose all their money. Some simply can't pull the trigger on a trade or investment. The opportunities slide right past them as they remain immobile and disappointed".

Most traders fail for two reasons: Fear of losing money and fear of failure.

The anecdote to this is to concentrate on the trading system itself and train oneself to focus only on the mechanics of trading. Think nothing of how much is being gained or lost. Only focus on the disciplined execution of your system. It's that simple.

The Zen of trading

Clearing ones mind of extraneous thought has been a key tenant of eastern religion for thousands of years. In today's world of "information saturation" we are constantly bombarded and overwhelmed by media of various sorts. Imagine if the ancients had problems clearing their minds, what would they have thought about modern times? But even more pervasive is the propensity for negative messages and idealistic images which are constantly pushed by advertising and news. A trader must not let their mind get cluttered by the constant distractions. More important, a trader must keep a positive and optimistic attitude. How does one do that?

There are numerous books on self improvement and spirituality that offer many methods and philosophies. As for the author, I found a very practical and effective system as expounded in The Handbook of Higher Consciousness by

Ram Dass. In his wonderful book, Dass makes the connection between emotion and programming the brain. We learn by a powerful combination of emotion coincidental with a learning experience. An example is when you are frightened or angry, we are at our most vulnerable to programming behavior because of the chemicals and hormones amplify behavior. That is why we sometimes act very irrationally because we were programmed when we were children and we keep responding to that infantile programming.

Dass recommends a very easy way to reprogram ourselves. We need to stimulate emotion at the same time we program instructions to our brain. He suggests that we cover out head with a pillow and scream into the pillow "no negative thinking" over and over again. The more emotion, the better. My friends, it works for me. When ever I get negative, it's to the "screaming pillow" I go. Maybe it will work for you.

Because of my need to keep positive in my trading (keep in mind that a trader may have almost as many losing trades as winners), I learned a valuable technique that helps me keep positive in all situations—all the time. Without my pillow, I would have probably been like most normal traders when going through a losing streak ... "lose my cool". When you lose your cool, fear and doubt can push you to abandon your system and lose your capital.

You may not need a pillow, but you should find a way to keep centered and positive. There's a lot of literature on the psychology of trading and investing. Believe me, understanding you-rself and how to "be above the fray" is as important as a good trading system. Moreover, your self-awareness will help you immensely in all aspects of your life.

Establishing healthy habit patterns

Some traders get mesmerized by their computer screens. It's the same kind of stupor that one sees in people watching reruns of "Green Acres". It is best to have a set time for trading and not get locked into sitting all day in front of the screen. Many traders believe that active trading usually takes place (in the USA) from opening to about 11am but many traders understand the movements of their favored investment vehicles and for that reason specialize in certain stocks or commodities.

It is natural when first starting to trade to want to be there to make sure that the nightmare scenario doesn't happen while one is away from the screen. But, if you have a good system with stop losses and good execution instructions, there should be no need to hover over the screen. In fact, it could be symptom of fear. Not only that, its easy to remotely monitor your positions. Try to carry on a routine where you spend as little time as possible in front of the screen. Find other ways to keep track of your positions. This will help relieve stress and allow more time to do research on your next trades or something that helps keep the tension below the awareness level.

As mentioned in the last section, it is a good idea to pay attention to your state of mind. Traders today have access to many resources that didn't exist only a few years ago. Today, traders can find personal coaches to help keep them "in tune". Professionals—even the best—seem to find that having a personal trainer is helpful. Tiger Woods is the best there is in his game, but relies heavily on a personal trainer to keep him "in the groove". There are numerous seminars, online courses and traders' blogs that allow other traders to come together and share information and experiences. If you plan to be a professional trader, take the attitude that you will act like one and constantly keep in training and challenging your-self to improve through education and communication with others in your profession.

Keeping a Journal

Record keeping is part of way we track our performance. Each trade should be documented and analyzed as to its success or failure. Was it the system or was it you? Keep a journal that not only tracks the mechanics of a trade but also take the time to analyze why you made the decisions you made. Were they emotional or technical? How would you have done things differently?

It's not that you are chronicling for future generations or to publish a book, the purpose is to make you take the time to analyze and write it down. If you actually write it down, you will help your cognitive process in learning from your actions.

If you find that you are following your system and it's just not working, then it's time to change the system. In this way, over time, you may evolve yourself and your trading system. Journaling also helps develop discipline and helps slow you down and hopefully keep you from repeating the same mistakes.

Build self-confidence

Remember that you can be successful and still have more losing trades than winning ones. It's a matter of cutting loses quickly and making sure that your winners are at least three times the amount of your losses. Learn to keep your confidence even when you are pulling the trigger on a bad trade. Each loss means you are closer to a win. Keep a positive attitude and stick by your system. Be as mechanical as you can and shut out any emotion or "hunches". Winning as a trader is a long-distance proposition.

Just as you don't ponder your losses, don't gloat over your successes. Analyze a good trade for the signals and elements that made it a winner. Try to recognize the repetition of the same elements in other winning trades. Be humble, cold, calculating and above all, never lose your cool. If you do, step back and take a break and analyze what took place technically as well as psychologically. Be hones in your self-appraisal. That's why it would be a good idea to have a personal coach or an online chat with other traders who understand what you are going through.

If you get to the minimum draw-down on your investment capital, pull out and reevaluate. There is always tomorrow and all successful traders have scars. If it were easy, everybody would be doing it and you aren't everybody.

Summary of Chapter 5

- The two main reasons for being unsuccessful at trading is: Fear of losing money and the fear of being wrong.
- One must not only learn the technical aspects of trading but also the proper trading psychology.
- Be disciplined and stick to your system.

- Keeping a positive attitude is key.
- Learn a technique for keeping positive.
- Constant education
- Keep a trading journal.
- Analyze every trade—technically and psychologically
- Consider having a personal coach or contact with other traders.
- Develop healthy tiding habits.
- Build self-confidence.
- Being successful at trading is a long distance proposition.
- Learn to step back and re-evaluate yourself and your system.

CHAPTER 6

Getting Started

You have been introduced to the concepts of trading options and an idea of what it takes to be an option trader. Trading options is not for passive investors. It takes not only an understanding of fundamental and technical analysis but also the concepts of developing a system and implementing it. Once you have this basic understanding, it's time to put what you've learned into practice.

"Wait a minute", you say. "I'm not ready to pony up the money until I feel more confident." Ok ... when will that be? Can we say, "fear of losing money or fear of being wrong".

Doing something new is always a bit intimidating but doing it with the chance of some financial (and some ego) pain is even more so. But before you plunge-in and start pulling out your wallet, why not practice first. So, we're going to do some virtual trades first.

Virtual Trading

Many stock brokerage houses now offer what is called "Virtual Trading". This is the next step you should take. A Virtual Trading account allows you to place trades as if you were actually making a trade. You even have to open an account and deposit real money but the trades you make are only "paper trades".

You begin doing your research and choosing an option to trade. You then call up your broker and he/she will help you place the trade. No trade will actually be made but you will go through the actual steps in placing a trade.

You will then track the trade and follow the rules for your system. If the price hits your stop-loss target, you'll call your broker to make sure that the position was closed out and record the paper loss plus paper commission in your journal. Or, if your trade goes the way planned (hoped?), you decide when to close out the position and then record the paper gain minus paper commission in your journal. You then analyze the trade as to technical and psychological observations and then figure out your net ROI for the trade. Then you do it again … and again.

How long should you do Virtual Trading?

When you do virtual trading, you are trying to accomplish several things:

- The mechanics of opening and closing a position
- How to record and analyze trades
- How well your system works (per cent winners)
- How well you like working with the brokerage.
- How you will schedule your trading activities.
- How well you like trading and if you want to continue.

Once you feel you have answered all of these items, you are ready to take off the "training wheels" and let the "real game" begin. I say "real game" because virtual trading is not really "virtual" because there is no real risk or reward.

The real benefit of virtual trading is that when you are in it for real, you don't have to worry about the mechanics and can focus on dominating your emotions-particularly when you lose.

Choosing a broker

Investment advisors and stock brokers are required to pass stringent exams and are closely supervised but it is the client's responsibility to understand the fiduciary relationship that exists and to know the rights of the investor.

The following is put out by the Securities and Exchange Commission: http://www.sec.gov/investor/pubs/invadvisers.htm

Investment Advisers: What You Need to Know Before Choosing One

The SEC receives many questions about investment advisers—what they are and how to go about choosing one. This document answers some of the typical questions we receive from investors about investment advisers. This Q&A is for the benefit of investors. You should not rely upon it to determine if you need to register as an investment adviser.

Q: What is an investment adviser?

A: Investment advisers are in the business of giving advice about securities to clients. For instance, individuals who receive compensation for giving advice to a specific person on investing in stocks, bonds, or mutual funds, are investment advisers. Some investment advisers manage portfolios of securities.

Q: What is the difference between an investment adviser and a financial planner?

A: Most financial planners are investment advisers, but not all investment advisers are financial planners. Some financial planners assess every aspect of your financial life—including saving, investments, insurance, taxes, retirement, and estate planning—and help you develop a detailed strategy or financial plan for meeting all your financial goals.

Others call themselves financial planners, but they may only be able to recommend that you invest in a narrow range of products, and sometimes products that aren't securities.

Before you hire any financial professional, you should know exactly what services you need, what services the professional can deliver, any limitations on what they can recommend, what services you're paying for, how much those services cost, and how the adviser or planner gets paid.

For information about the differences among brokers, investment advisers, and financial planners, read "Cutting Through the Confusion: Where to Turn for Help with Your Investments", which is available on the website of the North American Securities Administrators Association.

Q: What questions should I ask when choosing an investment adviser or financial planner?

A: Here are some of the questions you should always ask when hiring any financial professional:

- What experience do you have, especially with people in my circumstances?

- Where did you go to school? What is your recent employment history?
- What licenses do you hold? Are you registered with the SEC, a state, or the <u>NASD</u>?
- What products and services do you offer?
- Can you only recommend a limited number of products or services to me? If so, why?
- How are you paid for your services? What is your usual hourly rate, flat fee, or commission?
- Have you ever been disciplined by any government regulator for unethical or improper conduct or been sued by a client who was not happy with the work you did?
- For registered investment advisers, will you send me a copy of both parts of your Form ADV?

Be sure to meet potential advisers "face to face" to make sure you get along. And remember: there are many types of individuals who can help you develop a personal financial plan and manage your hard-earned money. The most important thing is that you know your financial goals, have a plan in place, and check out the professional you chose with your securities regulator.

Q: How do investment advisers get paid?

A: Before you hire any financial professional—whether it's a stockbroker, a financial planner, or an investment adviser—you should always find out and make sure you understand how that person gets paid. Investment advisers generally are paid in any of the following ways:

- A percentage of the value of the assets they manage for you;
- An hourly fee for the time they spend working for you;
- A fixed fee;
- A commission on the securities they sell; or
- Some combination of the above.

Each compensation method has potential benefits and possible drawbacks, depending on your individual needs. Ask the investment advisers you interview to explain the differences to you before you do business with them, and get several opinions before making your decision.

Q: Do investment advisers have to register with the U.S. Securities and Exchange Commission?

A: Depending on their size, investment advisers have to register with either the SEC or the state securities agency where they have their principal place of business. For the most part, investment advisers who manage $25 million or more in client assets must register with the SEC. If they manage less than $25 million, they must register with the state securities agency in the state where they have their principal place of business.

Q: How do I find out whether an investment adviser ever had problems with a government regulator or has a disciplinary history?

A: Most investment advisers must fill out a form called "Form ADV." They must file their ADVs with either the SEC or the state securities agency in the state where they have their principal place of business, depending on the amount of assets they manage.

The ADV consists of two parts. Part I contains information about the adviser's education, business, and whether they've had problems with regulators or clients. Part II outlines the adviser's services, fees, and strategies. Before you hire someone to be your investment adviser, always ask for, and carefully read, both parts of the ADV.

You can get copies of Form ADVs from the investment adviser, your state securities regulator, or the SEC, depending on the size of the adviser. You can find out how to get in touch with your state securities regulator through the North American Securities Administrators Association, Inc.'s Web site or by calling (202) 737-0900. Ask your state securities regulator whether they've had any complaints about the adviser, and ask them to check the CRD.

If the SEC registers the investment adviser, you can get the Form ADV at a cost of 24 cents per page (plus tax and postage) from the SEC at

> Office of Public Reference
> Room 1580
> 100 F Street, NE
> Washington, D.C. 20549-2521
> phone: (202) 551-8090
> fax: (202) 777-1027
> e-mail: publicinfo@sec.gov

Q: What should I do if the financial professional claims that he or she is "certified"?

A: If the professional you're considering claims to be a CFP® certificant, you should also visit the website of the <u>Certified Financial Planner Board of Standards, Inc.</u> to see if the professional is, in fact, certified as a CFP® professional and whether the professional's certification has been suspended or revoked by the CFP Board. You can also call the CFP Board at (888) 237-6275 to obtain other disciplinary information about the professional.

Q: Are investment advisers required to have credentials?

A: While some investment advisers and financial planners have credentials—such as CFP® certification or CFA (chartered financial analyst)—no state or federal law requires these credentials. Unlike federally registered advisers, many states do require their advisers and representatives to pass a proficiency exam or meet other requirements.

Investment advisers and financial planners may come from many different educational and professional backgrounds. Before you hire a financial professional, be sure to ask about their background. If they have a credential, ask them what it means and what they had to do to earn it. Also find out what organization issued the credential, and then contact the organization to verify whether the professional you're considering did, in fact, earn the credential and whether the professional remains in good standing with the organization. For information on various financial professional credentials and the entities that issue them, please visit NASD's website and read <u>Understanding Financial Professional Designations</u>.

Investor rights

The following is put out by the North American Securities Administration Association and helps to point out what the client should expect of an investment advisor/Stock Broker.[9]

---

9   nasaa.org.

Ask for and receive information from a firm about the work history and background of the person handling your account, as well as information about the firm itself.

Receive complete information about the risks, obligations, and costs of any investment before investing.

Receive recommendations consistent with your financial needs and investment objectives.

Receive a copy of all completed account forms and agreements.

Receive account statements that are accurate and understandable.

Understand the terms and conditions of transactions you undertake.

Access your funds in a timely manner and receive information about any restrictions or limitations on access.

Discuss account problems with the branch manager or compliance department of the firm and receive prompt attention to and fair consideration of your concerns.

Receive complete information about commissions, sales charges, maintenance or service charges, transaction or redemption fees, and penalties.

Contact your state or provincial securities agency in order to verify the employment and disciplinary history of a securities salesperson and the salesperson's firm; find out if the investment is permitted to be sold; or file a complaint.

Full service vs. Discount brokerage accounts

Whether full service or discount, as a new option trader, you should have the opportunity to do virtual trading with any potential broker you choose. This should be the first consideration: does the service provider have a virtual trading program?

In the past, investors and traders needed research to help make investment decisions. But in recent times, the internet has made it possible for the "do-it-yourself investor to have access to much of the same information that a full service brokerage can offer. Naturally because of the added cost of employing highly trained and highly paid analysts, and developing the retail aspects of marketing full service, the traditional brokerage houses must charge higher commissions than the basic services offered by the online discount brokerages. For those with the knowledge and time, Discount brokerages offer lower costs and enhance profit margins on trades. A no brainer—for the experienced or long term investor who does a little research and holds a position for a long time. There are also some other things that need to be taken into consideration.

For active traders, execution is vital. This can be a concern for those using discount or online accounts. For many traders, having someone to talk to is reassuring and helps give some valuable feedback with a history attached. For many traders and investors, it's important to develop a relationship with a broker. It's an interpersonal need that many humans feel a need to have a consistent chain of communication when transacting any sort of business. Others, however, feel little need. It depends on the individual trader.

Another factor to keep in mind is that technology is wonderful—as long as it works. If you need to make a trade or close out a position, there is nothing more frustrating than to have problems with your connection with the net or hardware problems. It gives Murphy's law fertile ground to operate and can cost you money. But, many online and discount brokerages have done a good job at moving to the center by offering a carte blanche menu of services which allows traders to tailor their needs and control trading costs.

There is no getting away from the fact that commission costs are a major factor in signing up, but as a new options trader, it probably worth the extra costs to go with a full service brokerage until you feel confident to go more on your own. Not only will you get the advantage of experience, a research department and some hand holding, but also you can get some objective feedback as you learn and test your system. Moreover, even if your broker is not a specialist in trading options, there is usually a department which does specialize and you can tap into this resource, as well.

Many of the full service brokerages are starting to offer a spectrum of prices for service and it might be a good idea to hook up with a brokerage that can help scale back your trading costs as you grow more competent and confident.

If you decide to go with a discount broker, be sure to check annual surveys to see which firms offer the best service (Barron's Magazine and Smart Money Magazine are worth checking out). Often times you get what you pay for, so try not to let price be the total determining factor. Service and trade execution are very important as well. You may find a broker that charges a $5 commission, but if their website is down or brokers aren't answering the phone when you need to place a trade (which has happened to me) you can lose a lot more money on the actual transaction than you are saving in commission costs.

If you would like to receive one-stop shopping for all of your financial needs, then a full service broker may make sense. You will pay for it in the form of higher costs, but that convenience can give you peace of mind, which is worth a lot.

When interviewing a potential service provider, make sure to tell them that you want to trade options, that you are new at it, and ask them about what resources they have dedicated to supporting option traders. It's also a good idea to ask the manager of the brokerage office to hook you up with a broker who is experienced in trading options before you interview with any individual broker; they all want your business.

Can you keep a secret?

For many, this can be the hardest thing to do.

I recommend that you not discuss your trading with anybody—particularly your spouse—but for the exception of your broker or others in "the Biz". Don't brag and don't whine. You should be all about "following a system" and not about your genius or misfortune.

The best way to keep emotions out of your trading is not making being an options trader part of your "image". It's just another business, but without the aggravation of clients or employees. It's all in your head and the fewer people who know about what you do the better. It's just easier to keep control of your emotions if you keep others out. But, I repeat, it is important to talk with other traders or a personal coach. You can play the lonely hero; waging the silent battle to do your own special thing in the world. It's definitely not for everybody.

The following is an article found at TradingSuccessRoadmap.com and is worthy of sharing with all new traders.

Characteristics of Successful Traders

Many investors take actions that aren't in their best self-interest. They make irrational trades; they trade based on emotion, rather than logic; they hold on to a losing position due to their unwillingness to admit they made a bad trade; they trade based on greed or panic ... the list is endless.

Successful traders, on the other hand, all have a few things in common. Developing these characteristics and habits will help make you a successful trader.

Successful Traders Set Goals

Successful traders tend to be incredibly goal-oriented. Why? Most people perform at their best when they're reaching for a *clear* goal. And there are three basic qualities that make up a clear goal:

- The goal must be realistic. If your goal is to double your money every day, it sounds great—but it's not realistic.
- The goal must be attainable. Just like with a realistic goal, an attainable goal must be within your current capabilities. The best goals are short-term goals; make your first goal a small one, and then continue to increase your goals as you experience success. World-class sprinters don't start by thinking of winning the Olympics.
- The goal must be measurable. Goals that aren't precise, and can't be quantified or measured, aren't really goals at all. If your goal is to be wealthy, that's great ... but what does "wealthy" mean? Our guess is that your definition of "wealth" will change as your net worth increases. If you can't define your goal, and measure your progress towards it,

then you have no way of assessing your progress or of making changes to your techniques and strategies that allow you to reach your goal.

Successful traders set goals, and they also are confident they can reach their goals. Confidence is a key to staying rational, logical, and disciplined. Starting with small, realistic goals will help build your confidence in yourself and your abilities.

Success Can Come at Any Level

Whether you're a beginning trader, a trader with some experience, or someone who makes his or her living strictly from trading, you can be successful. Many people think they have to have significant capital, or years of experience, to trade successfully. That's not true. (It's also true that if you don't stay disciplined, focused, and rational, you'll end up as a losing trader, regardless of your level of "expertise.") All successful traders started as small investors; they didn't trade more than they could safely risk, they learned from their mistakes, and they developed systems that worked for them and that fit their personal styles. We have not defined different strategies for different "levels" of traders in this book because the principles are the same: logical, focused, disciplined trading creates success.

Successful Traders Specialize

It's simply not possible to understand and stay in touch with everything that occurs in all the types of investment vehicles and markets across the world. While some traders have developed systems that allow them to trade in multiple venues (for instance, in different stock markets around the world), most traders specialize in a particular type of investment, and in a particular market. You may enjoy trading in commodities futures; that enjoyment will help you focus and stay in touch with market events. If you aren't interested in currency trading, for example, don't trade in it—your lack of knowledge and motivation will cause you to lose focus and make mistakes. Successful traders tend to specialize; they pick an area to gain in-depth knowledge of, and they follow it closely, learning from past trends and patterns, and from their own trades. If you're a beginning trader, we recommend focusing narrowly on a particular investment vehicle and market; learn all you can, about the market and about yourself, before you move into other investment types.

Successful Traders Take Losses in Stride

No one likes to lose. But losing is a fact of life for traders; the key is to limit your losses and maximize your successes.

A losing trade is not a failure. It isn't a reflection of you or of your overall judgment. (If it was possible to be right every time, we'd all be rich.) The only way a losing trade is truly a failure is if you aren't willing to take the loss, without hesitation, and move on to find winning trades. By accepting that they've made a losing trade, and getting out of the position, successful traders focus on making money—not on being right all the time.

Many traders feel they don't want to "lose" money on any trade, and they stay in losing positions in the hopes that it will recover to at least the break-even point. There are three problems with this approach:

1. The position may never recover to the break-even point.
2. Holding on to a losing position ties up capital that could be placed into winning trades.
3. Holding on to a losing position is an example of unfocused trading and a lack of discipline.

Successful traders are willing to take small losses. If you aren't willing to take small losses, or don't have the discipline to take small losses, don't trade.

Successful Traders Stay Focused During Rapid Swings

Most of us were raised to think that it takes years of hard work to acquire wealth. That viewpoint doesn't apply to trading in the markets; you can make thousands of dollars in minutes under the right circumstances. Successful traders understand that money can be made or lost extremely quickly, and they stay calm and rational.

Why is that attitude important? Let's say you've made several thousand dollars over the course of an hour trading futures contracts. You're thrilled and excited, and you may lose your composure and start making irrational trades. You may stay in the position longer than you should, for one of two reasons:

- You think the market will keep going up, and you don't want to limit your gains.
- The market falls, and you don't want to give up all the gains you've made, so you hold on in hopes your position will rally.

If you accept and understand that huge amounts of money can be made in a short period of time, you are less likely to become undisciplined in your trading. Successful traders take their gains in stride, no matter how large. They quickly move to protect their positions by setting stops, or covering a percentage of a short position. Successful traders stay rational and disciplined in the face of rapid gains or losses because they understand the nature of trading.

Successful Traders Stay Flexible

Staying flexible requires that you stay detached and unemotional about your trades. No matter how strongly you feel about your analysis of a position or a trade, you have to be willing to change that opinion and act quickly if necessary.

Successful traders realize that bad trades reduce the gains made from past trades and potential gains from future trades. Successful traders change their minds quickly and easily, and are not concerned about whether they were "right" or "wrong." They're concerned with maximizing their gains and minimizing their losses—and to minimize losses, they have to be willing to quickly change their minds.

Remember: the more flexible you are, the more successful you will be.

Successful Traders Don't Leap Before They Look

One of the most common mistakes inexperienced traders make is to trade when they see an opportunity they think *might* be too good to miss. Jumping into a position based on a hunch, or on the belief that you may be missing an opportunity, is no different than gambling. Almost every investor at one time or another has felt a rush of greed or enthusiasm for a trade-based solely on the desire not to miss out on a great opportunity that *might* be available.

Successful traders practice self-discipline, and apply skill and logic to their trading. They learn every day, and they use what they know to make intelligent decisions on every trade. Successful traders don't worry about missing out—they focus on making intelligent decisions.

Successful Traders Don't Passively Follow "Expert" Advice

Blindly following the investment advice of a broker or analyst is foolish and self-destructive. Oftentimes, the broker's self-interest is completely different from yours, because the broker gets paid when you make a trade, whether it's a good trade or not. He or she *wants* you to trade. Analysts may have inside knowledge or years worth of experience, but in the end their opinions on the markets are just that—opinions.

Successful traders take responsibility for their trades and therefore their money. They learn, they stay focused and disciplined, and they make their *own* judgments about their trades.

CHAPTER 7

Putting It All Together

Seven days. Roughly ten pages per day and now you're ready to move from the realm of ideas to reality. Of course, if it took you more than seven days, that shows that you, indeed, have a life. But if you have finished this introduction to trading stock options, you are probably going to go the next step. Hang on, it's a fun ride. And if you follow the postulates of this book, you will make money. It all depends on you, dear reader. But I know you can do it. I did.

Here are your next steps

1. To keep the momentum going, start your search for a good broker and a wire house that will let you do virtual trading. Plan on starting your virtual trading within seven days (a little symmetry never hurts).

2. Re read Chapters 1–4. Make sure you understand everything.

3. Set up your first trading journal page. See example below:

date of trade	symbol	# contracts	open price	total $	close price	total $	fees	net profit/ loss$	%

Trade comments:

date of trade	symbol	# contracts	open price	total $	close price	total $	fees	net profit/ loss$	%

Trade comments:

Remember, trading is all about *discipline* and you should cut no corners—including your journal. Do it religiously.

4. Choose or develop a system for trading. Your have several choices:

   • You can lean upon your brokerage's option research department for recommendations and your broker for ideas on his/her system (if they are experienced and also trade on their own. Remember, it's easy to give advice when it's not your money.)

   • Use the method discussed in this book

   • Research for online advisory services. But make sure you fully understand the system they use and know their track record.

   • Research and purchase of software trading system.

   There may be other alternatives, but whatever you do, be disciplined in which ever system you choose. During your period of virtual trading, you might want to try several systems and pick the one best for you.

5. Once you have chosen a system, write out each step in checklist form.

6. Read over the chapter on Trading Psychology-pages (57–60) and review the article on "Characteristics of a successful trader" (66–68).

7. Write out "I realize that I am going to have losses, but I understand the nature of the game and know that I will be successful over the long run." Put this statement where you can see it every day.

8. Once you have done these things, you are as prepared as you'll ever be … so, it's time to "rock and roll".

9. For Stock and Stock Options picks go to ThinkNTrade.com.

Glossary

Accredited Investor

Term used by SEC in Regulation D of private placements. Concept: although 35 is the upper limit of persons who may purchase a private placement, accredited investors are not included in this number. General definition of accredited investors: institutional type accounts and persons of wealth (persons with a net worth of $1 Million or more, persons with annual income of $200,000 or more, persons who purchase $150,000 or more of the offering and this does not represent more than 20% of their net worth).

Alpha

A measure of the residual risk that an investor takes for investing in a fund rather than a market index. It represents the difference between a mutual fund's actual performance and the performance that would be expected based on the level of risk taken by the fund's manager. If a fund produced the expected return for the level of risk assumed, the fund would have an Alpha of zero. A positive Alpha indicates the manager produced a return greater than expected for the risk taken. A negative Alpha indicates the manager has not adequately rewarded investors for the risks taken.

AMEX

The term used for the American Stock Exchange.

Ask

Also known as the "offer", the price that the market maker guarantees to fill a buy order. A buy order placed at the market will usually be filled at the current asking (offer) price. The ask price is usually greater than the bid price.

Back Testing

A strategy that is optimized on historical data, then applied to current data to see if the results are similar. Rarely done properly and usually resorts to a form of curve fitting.

Bar Chart

A popular way to display and analyze financial price information in graphical form. The horizontal axis of a bar chart represents the passage of time with the most recent time periods on the right side while the vertical axis represents the stock's price.

Basing

A period where the stock or market is "catching its breath" after a decline, characterized by a flat trading range without any noticeable trend. It is common to see a basing period after a lengthy decline of the stock price. Basing may be a sign of accumulation.

Basis

The difference between cash prices and the futures contract prices.

Bear

A person who believes prices will decline and might be described as having a "bearish" outlook. Bear markets occur when roughly 80% of all stocks decline for an extended period of time. 1973–74 and 1981–82 have been referred to as bear markets.

Bear Market

A long period of time when prices in the market are generally declining. It is often measured by a percentage decline of more than 20%.

Bid

The price at which the market maker guarantees to fill a sell order. A sell order placed at the market will usually be filled at the current bid price. The bid price is usually less than the ask price.

Bollinger Bands

An indicator that allows users to compare volatility and relative price levels over a period of time. It consists of three bands designed to encompass the majority of a security's price action. Prices will often meet resistance at the upper band and support at the lower band.

Breakout

Price of a security emerging from a previous trading pattern. The new price "breaks out" above the high (or below the low) trading pattern lines that enclose all other prices for that security in the preceding period. Breakouts are used by technical analysts to predict substantial upside or downside movement.

Bull

A person who believes prices will advance and might be described as having a "bullish" outlook. Bull markets occur when roughly 80% of all stocks advance over an extended period of time. 1982–87 and 1995–99 have been referred to as bull markets.

Buy Signal

A condition that indicates a good time to buy a stock. The exact circumstances of the signal will be determined by the indicator that an analyst is using. For example, it's considered a buy signal when the <u>MACD</u> crosses above its signal line.

Buy Stop

A buy order usually placed above the current price, ensuring that a security would have to trade at the set level before the buy order would be activated. at 35. By placing a buy stop order just above <u>resistance</u>, a trader can ensure that the security will break resistance before going long. On the other hand, traders looking to catch a bottom or intraday low might place a buy stop below the current price, but near <u>support</u>.

Buyback

A company's repurchase of it's own shares of stock.

Call

An Option contract that gives the holder the right to buy the underlying security at a specified price for a certain, fixed period of time. *See also <u>Put</u>.*

Cash Settlement

The process by which the terms of an option contract are fulfilled through the payment or receipt in dollars of the amount by which the option is in-the-money as opposed to delivering or receiving the underlying stock.

CBOE

The Chicago Board Options Exchange; the first national exchange to trade listed stock options.

Closing Purchase

A transaction in which the purchaser's intention is to reduce or eliminate a short position in a given series of options

Closing Sale

A transaction in which the seller's intention is to reduce or eliminate a long position in a given series of options

Closing Transaction

A trade that reduced an investor's position. Closing buy transactions reduce short positions and closing sell transactions reduce long positions

Contingent Order

An order which can be executed only if another event occurs; i.e. "sell Oct 45 call 7.25 with stock 52 or lower".

Covered Call

An option strategy in which a call option is written against long stock on a share-for-share basis.

Covered Call Option Writing

A strategy in which one sells call options while simultaneously owning an equivalent position in the underlying security or strategy in which one sells put options and simultaneously is short an equivalent position in the underlying security.

Debit

An expense, or money paid out from an account. A debit transaction is one in which the net cost is greater than the net sale proceeds

Delta

The amount by which an option's price will change for a one-point change in price by the underlying entity. Call options have positive deltas, while put options have negative deltas. Technically, the delta is an instantaneous measure of the option's price change, so that the delta will be altered for even fractional changes by the underlying entity

Early Exercise (assignment)

The exercise or assignment of an option contract before its expiration date.

Exercise

To implement the right under which the holder of an option is entitled to buy (in the case of a call) or sell (in the case of a put) the underlying security.

Exercise price

The price at which the option holder may buy or sell the underlying security, as defined in the terms of his option contract. It is the price at which the call holder may exercise to buy the underlying security or the put holder may exercise to sell the underlying security. For listed options, the exercise price is the same as the Striking Price.

Expiration date

The day on which an option contract becomes void. The expiration date for listed stock options is the Saturday after the third Friday of the expiration month. Holders of options should indicate their desire to exercise, if they wish to do so, by this date.

Expiration time

The time of day by which all exercise notices must be received on the expiration date. Technically, the expiration time is currently 5:00PM on the expiration date, but public holders of option contracts must indicate their desire to exercise no later than 5:30PM on the business day preceding the expiration date. The times are Eastern Time

Fair Value

Normally, a term used to describe the worth of an option or futures contract as determined by a mathematical model. Also sometimes used to indicate intrinsic value

Float

The number of shares outstanding of a particular common stock.

Implied Volatility

A measure of the volatility of the underlying stock, it is determined by using option prices currently existing in the market at the time rather than using historical data on the price changes of the underlying stock.

Index

A compilation of the prices of several common entities into a single number.

Index Option

An option whose underlying entity is an index. Most index options are cash-based.

In-the-money

A term describing any option that has intrinsic value. A call option is in-the-money if the underlying security is higher than the striking price of the call. A put option is in-the-money if the security is below the striking price.

Intrinsic value

The value of an option if it were to expire immediately with the underlying stock at its current price; the amount by which an option is in-the-money. For call options, this is the difference between the stock price and the striking price, if that difference is a positive number, or zero otherwise. For put options it is the difference between the striking price and the stock price, if that difference is positive, and zero otherwise.

Last Trading Day

The very last full day of open trading before an options expiration day, usually the third Friday of the expiration month.

Limit Order

An order to buy or sell securities at a specified price (the limit). A limit order may also be placed "with discretion". In this case, the floor broker executing the order may use his (her) discretion to buy or sell at a set amount beyond the limit if he (she) feels it is necessary to fill the order.

Long Position

A position wherein an investor's interest in a particular series of options is as a net holder (i.e., the number of contracts bought exceeds the number of contracts sold).

Margin

To buy a security by borrowing funds from a brokerage house. The margin requirement—the maximum percentage of the investment that can be loaned by the brokerage firm—is set by the Federal Reserve Board.

Market-Maker

An exchange member whose function is to aid in the making of a market, by making bids and offers for his account in the absence of public buy or sell orders. Several market-makers are normally assigned to a particular security. The market-maker system encompasses the market-makers, floor brokers, and order book office

Market Order

An order to buy or sell securities at the current market. The order will be filled as long as there is a market for the security.

Opening Purchase

A transaction in which the purchaser's intention is to create or increase a long position in a given series of options.

Opening Sale

A transaction in which the seller's intention is to create or increase a short position in a given series of options.

Opening Transaction

A trade which adds to the net position of an investor. An opening buy transaction adds more long securities to the account. An opening sell transaction adds more short securities.

Open Interest

The number of outstanding option contracts in the exchange market or in a particular class or series.

Out-of-the-money

A call option is out-of-the-money if the strike price is greater than the market price of the underlying security. A put option is out-of-the-money if the strike price is less than the market price of the underlying security.

Overvalued

Describing a security trading at a higher price than it logically should. Normally associated with the results of option price predictions by mathematical models. If an option is trading in the market for a higher price than the model indicates, the option is said to be overvalued.

Position

As a noun, specific securities in an account or strategy. (A covered call writing position might be long 1,000 XYZ and short 10 XYZ January 30 calls). As a verb, to facilitate; to buy or sell—generally a block of securities—thereby establishing a position.

Put

An option contract that gives the holder the right to sell the underlying security at a specified price for a certain fixed period of time.

Resistance

A term in technical analysis indicating a price area higher than the current stock price where an abundance of supply exists for the stock and therefore the stock may have trouble rising through the price.

Return (on investment)

The percentage profit that one makes, or might make, on his investment.

Return if Exercised

The return that a covered call writer would make if the underlying stock were called away.

Settlement Price

The official price at the end of a trading session. This price is established by The Options Clearing Corporation and is used to determine changes in account equity, margin requirements, and for other purposes.

Short Position

A position wherein a person's interest in a particular series of options is as a net writer (i.e., the number of contracts sold exceeds the number of contracts bought).

Stop Order

An order, placed away from the current market, that becomes a market order if the security trades at the price specified on the stop order. Buy stop orders are placed above the market while sell stop orders are placed below.

Strategy

With respect to option investments, a preconceived, logical plan of position selection and follow-up action.

Strike Price

The stated price per share for which the underlying security may be purchased (in the case of a call) or sold (in the case of a put) by the option holder upon exercise of the option contract.

Support

A term in technical analysis indicating a price area lower than the current price of the stock, where demand is thought to exist. Thus a stock would stop declining when it reached a support area.

Technical Analysis

The method of predicting future stock price movements based on observation of historical stock price movements.

Terms

The collective name denoting the expiration date, striking price, and underlying stock of an option contract.

Trader

An investor or professional who makes frequent purchases and sales.

978-0-595-45729-8
0-595-45729-0

www.ingramcontent.com/pod-product-compliance
Lightning Source LLC
Chambersburg PA
CBHW030845180526
45163CB00004B/1449